We recently lost our beloved pet "Bear," who was not only our best and dearest friend but also the "Vice President of Sunshine" here at Atlantic Publishing. He did not receive a salary but worked tirelessly 24 hours a day to please his parents. Bear was a rescue dog that turned around and showered myself, my wife Sherri, his grandparents Jean, Bob and Nancy and every person and animal he met (maybe not rabbits) with friendship and love. He made a lot of people smile every day.

We wanted you to know that a portion of the profits of this book will be donated to The Humane Society of the United States.

–Douglas & Sherri Brown

THE HUMANE SOCIETY
OF THE UNITED STATES©

The human-animal bond is as old as human history. We cherish our animal companions for their unconditional affection and acceptance. We feel a thrill when we glimpse wild creatures in their natural habitat or in our own backyard.

Unfortunately, the human-animal bond has at times been weakened. Humans have exploited some animal species to the point of extinction.

The Humane Society of the United States makes a difference in the lives of animals here at home and worldwide. The HSUS is dedicated to creating a world where our relationship with animals is guided by compassion. We seek a truly humane society in which animals are respected for their intrinsic value, and where the human-animal bond is strong.

Want to help animals? We have plenty of suggestions. Adopt a pet from a local shelter, join The Humane Society and be a part of our work to help companion animals and wildlife. You will be funding our educational, legislative, investigative and outreach projects in the U.S. and across the globe.

Or perhaps you'd like to make a memorial donation in honor of a pet, friend or relative? You can through our Kindred Spirits program. And if you'd like to contribute in a more structured way, our Planned Giving Office has suggestions about estate planning, annuities, and even gifts of stock that avoid capital gains taxes.

Maybe you have land that you would like to preserve as a lasting habitat for wildlife. Our Wildlife Land Trust can help you. Perhaps the land you want to share is a backyard—that's enough. Our Urban Wildlife Sanctuary Program will show you how to create a habitat for your wild neighbors.

So you see, it's easy to help animals. And The HSUS is here to help.

The Humane Society of the United States
2100 L Street NW
Washington, DC 20037
202-452-1100
www.hsus.org

The

Restaurant

Manager's Success

Chronicles

Insider Secrets and Techniques Food
Service Managers Use Every Day to
Make Millions

By Angela C. Adams, B.A.

The Restaurant Manager's Success Chronicles:
Insider Secrets and Techniques Food Service Managers Use Every Day
to Make Millions

ISBN-13: 978-0-910627-96-2   ISBN-10: 0-910627-96-7

Library of Congress Cataloging-in-Publication Data

Adams, Angela C., 1983-
  The restaurant manager's success chronicles : insider secrets and
techniques food service managers use every day to make millions by
Angela C. Adams.
      p. cm.
  Includes bibliographical references and index.
  ISBN-13: 978-0-910627-96-2
  ISBN-10: 0-910627-96-7
  1. Restaurant management--Case studies. 2. Restaurateurs--Interviews.
I. Title.

TX911.3.M27A228 2008
647.95068--dc22
                    2007049096

LIMIT OF LIABILITY/DISCLAIMER OF WARRANTY: The publisher and the author make no representations
or warranties with respect to the accuracy or completeness of the contents of this work and specifically
disclaim all warranties, including without limitation warranties of fitness for a particular purpose. No
warranty may be created or extended by sales or promotional materials. The advice and strategies contained
herein may not be suitable for every situation. This work is sold with the understanding that the publisher
is not engaged in rendering legal, accounting, or other professional services. If professional assistance is
required, the services of a competent professional should be sought. Neither the publisher nor the author
shall be liable for damages arising herefrom. The fact that an organization or Web site is referred to in this
work as a citation and/or a potential source of further information does not mean that the author or the
publisher endorses the information the organization or Web site may provide or recommendations it may
make. Further, readers should be aware that Internet Web sites listed in this work may have changed or
disappeared between when this work was written and when it is read.

Printed on Recycled Paper

INTERIOR DESIGN: Vickie Taylor • vtaylor@atlantic-pub.com

Printed in the United States

Author

Dedication

I would like to dedicate this book to all the managers who participated in this book.

I would also like to dedicate this book to Dennis who helped keep me motivated when I was crazy busy with everything going on. If it wasn't for him I am not sure I would have made it through this book.

Table of Contents

Section 2: What Those Managers Taught Us .. 171

Chapter 1: The Employees 173

Foreword

By Roy Assad

Being a restaurant manager is one of the most challenging responsibilities you can undertake. Diners today are expecting more, and consider dinning out a favorite pastime. Millions of people dine out daily, and it is the manager's responsibility to ensure that they have a great experience at your establishment.

You are the orchestra leader, the conductor; your symphony is the staff you hire, and the outcome is how you train and motivate them. You are the peacemaker, the leader; you are responsible for everything that goes on in the restaurant you manage, from the moment the guest walks in the door to the moment they walk out. Every little detail matters; how they were greeted, seated, served, and most importantly, handled, if complaints arise.

Everyday is a wedding, every guest is a VIP, and every meal needs to be perfect. As the referee between the front and back of the house, the entire restaurant responsibility rests squarely on your shoulders. With all this being said, this is one of the most rewarding positions to be in, if you love hospitality. You ensure that a birthday party goes without a hitch or an anniversary dinner is memorable.

This handbook is filled with so many great ideas. Some of these ideas are proven methodologies that have been in practice for a long time and some are new. You will find this an invaluable guide to creating a great experience at your restaurant every time!

To have a great dining experience, hundreds of things must go right. You will find the secret to all these little items that many managers miss. Reading this is a MUST!

Now, the ball is squarely in your court – read, absorb, learn, practice, and above all, create a memorable dining experience for every guest that visits your establishment!

About Roy Assad

Roy Assad is a professional advisor, motivational speaker, and executive coach. With nearly thirty years experience in an award winning sales career, he has mastered the arts of networking, negotiation and bridge-building. These skills have enhanced his effectiveness in the coaching of executives and entrepreneurs.

In 1990, he formed Rainmaker Strategies, a motivational speaking firm. Roy's unique insight into the dynamics of relationships and his desire to share this knowledge with others is the propelling force behind successful coaching and training. Roy coaches' executives and teams in uncovering key problem areas, identifying trigger points and, ultimately, eliminating roadblocks. Together with his client, Roy builds a solution-based strategy that will free them to overcome obstacles, unleash hidden potential and capitalize on the unique talents they possess with a focus on maximizing personal and professional success. Key to Roy's success are his innate interest in people, his ability to recognize their mental blocks and inefficiencies, and his skill in guiding their personal and career development.

Introduction

This book was compiled and written for those out there that are in the restaurant management industry or those that aspire to be. Read the stories of the people who have been in the business for many years. My hope is that you will learn from them; that you will take their backgrounds, their current careers, and their styles of management and you will be encouraged and inspired to do something great with your current management career or the management career you have in your future. Walk with them through their pasts and on to their goals for the future. Among that, take a peek into their restaurants.

Each manager's interview begins with their name and contact information. You will then be given a little background about the person, followed by information about their career, both past and present. These managers were asked numerous questions to dig right to the heart of their career and find out what would be beneficial for you to read and take something from. Some of the topics they were asked about were lessons they learned, management styles, management qualities, changes implemented, and their goals for the future.

After reading about these things, you will dive into a whole mix of management styles. These managers were asked over 40 questions about how their restaurant is run, including information about food, dealing with customers, recordkeeping, pricing, staff, and much more.

Finally, you will find the "Advice Tidbit." These managers gave some advice that they feel those who are already in restaurant management and those who are going to be in restaurant management will find useful.

I hope these stories will touch you and teach you all at the same time, just as they did with me.

Section

1

Success Stories

"The minimum time spent in any one restaurant should be a year, no matter what. You may feel that you're done earlier, but it's truly in a year that you learn the discipline and technical things you need to know about a particular restaurant."

~Mario Batali

"A successful man is one who can lay a firm foundation with the bricks others have thrown at him."

~David Brinkley

"Always bear in mind that your own resolution to succeed is more important than any other."

~Abraham Lincoln

"Success is dependent on effort."

~Sophocles

"What is success? I think it is a mixture of having a flair for the thing that you are doing; knowing that it is not enough, that you have got to have hard work and a certain sense of purpose."

~Margaret Thatcher

"Success is to be measured not so much by the position that one has reached in life as by the obstacles which he has overcome. "

~Booker T. Washington

Ali Amundson

Company	Uncorked — The Unpretentious Wine Bar
Address	16427 N. Scottsdale Rd. Ste. 130 Scottsdale, AZ 85254
Role in Company	Owner / Managing Member / Operator
E-mail	Under "Contact Us" on the Web site
Web site	**www.uncorkedwinebar.com**
Phone	480-699-9230
Fax	480-699-9239

Background

Ali Amundson has been in the restaurant industry for 20 years and in restaurant management for 7 years. She worked in many other restaurants before the restaurant she owns, Uncorked — The Unpretentious Wine Bar. Her first job in the hospitality industry was as a salad bar stocker and cashier at a Sizzler Steak House when she was a junior in high school. She decided to become a restaurant manager because of her personal and professional drive to move up in companies. Uncorked opened in October 2005, a year after she married her husband, Tim.

"Although opening a restaurant in your first year of marriage is not recommended, it helps to have an understanding husband like Tim!"

Career

Ali now owns her own restaurant, Uncorked — The Unpretentious Wine Bar, where she manages seven employees. Her ideal employee possesses the ability to be on time, has an outstanding work ethic, and a pride in what they do. She believes being able to multitask and delegate responsibilities is what it takes to be a good manager. Her qualities that help in her management career are being very hands on and setting a good example by doing everything she asks of her employees. Her specific management style is to watch and observe and then make suggestions that will help correct situations. Something unique she does when managing is to work with her employees instead of only having them work for her.

The toughest lesson Ali has learned so far in her management career is that, when you are on salary rather than hourly pay, you end up working way over 45 hours every week. When she first started in management, she wishes someone had told her not to be a pushover or let her employees walk all over her. She was not really given any advice when she started in management.

Ali is very proud of her wine bar, which she managed to open at the age of 38 after six years of planning. Her estimated sales from 2006 were $320,000. Her goal for the next five or ten years is to have her wine bar be successful financially, as well as being able to expand or sell her business.

A Little Restaurant Information

Uncorked — The Unpretentious Wine Bar serves bistro type food that goes well with wine. The restaurant is open Monday through Wednesday from 11 a.m. to 10 p.m., Thursday from 11 a.m. to 11 p.m., and Friday and Saturday from 11 a.m. to midnight. It is closed on Sunday. Their busiest hour varies everyday and every week. Reservations are accepted, but they do not have valet parking available. They serve wine, beer, and non-alcoholic beverages (soda, coffee, tea, and bottled water to name a few). They also offer the full menu to go and catering.

According to Ali, the cozy atmosphere and great service are what set the restaurant apart and draw in clientele. She says it is like being in your own living room. They also offer one television in the restaurant. The age group that seems to recommend the restaurant is 25 to 55.

The restaurant's food arrives fresh on a daily basis, and Ali handpicks the produce from local grocers. Pricing has never had to be adjusted due to competition, and their customer checks do not include gratuity. She has found the best way to keep costs down is by weekly inventory control and keeping food and wine spoil and waste sheets.

When it comes to her staff, the most important trait Ali looks for is a superstar work ethic. She has had to step in for her staff before. Being a small establishment she does it all. There is not an official host or hostess on staff, but everyone who is working greets each person who walks through the door. Bouncers are not needed for the restaurant. The staff is required to follow a dress code of black tops and black pants or jeans. Men are not required to wear ties.

Outside companies are hired to do accounting and payroll for the restaurant. They use a P.O.S. (Point of Sale) system to print the reports of daily records. Dishes are cleaned with a high temperature under-counter dishwasher.

Although they do not reward frequent diners, they will sometimes give their regular customers a percent off their bill. Coupons are offered in advertising (the Savvy Shopper).

Ali says that Uncorked — The Unpretentious Wine Bar has fulfilled her dream of what it should be, even though she would like it to be twice as busy. When asked if she would do it all over again if she had the chance, Ali said yes, but only if she had more money to work with in the beginning.

Advice Tidbits

"I don't know about managers, but for potential restaurant owners, I would say don't even entertain the fact of opening your own place unless you do years of research and know a lot about the business, preferably working in it for several years! It is so much more than investing a lot of money, hiring employees, and opening the doors.

"It is also best to concentrate a large part of your efforts on constantly coming up with new ways to build your business and keep increasing sales. It is very important to keep your "regulars" coming back — they are what will "make or break" your business."

Roy B. Assad

Company	Leila Restaurant
Address	120 S. Dixie Highway West Palm Beach, FL 33401
Role in Company	Managing Partner (Owner)
E-mail	roy@leilawpb.com
Web site	**www.leilawpb.com**
Phone	561-659-7373
Fax	561-833-9417

Background

Roy B. Assad has been in management for 15 years, in the restaurant industry for three years, and in restaurant management for all three years. Besides Leila, Roy also owned and operated L'Opera Brasserie. He decided to become a restaurant manager because he owned the restaurant.

Roy is a professional advisor, motivational speaker, and executive coach. With nearly 30 years experience in an award-winning sales career, he has mastered the arts of networking, negotiation, and bridge-building. These skills have enhanced his effectiveness in the coaching of executives and entrepreneurs.

In 1990, Roy formed Rainmaker Strategies, a motivational speaking firm. Today he is a partner in the Human Capital Group, a four member executive coaching and consulting firm, and a managing partner/owner in Leila Restaurant, both of which are located in West Palm Beach, Florida. He also participates in numerous boards and committees and holds positions in some of them. These include: Board Chairman, Downtown Development Authority of West Palm Beach; Board of Directors, Conventions & Visitors Bureau; and Board Member, Cystic Fibrosis Foundation.

His areas of expertise are personal development, leadership training, effective networking, art of negotiation, emotional intelligence, communication skills, financial coaching, sales training, keynote addresses, and strategic thinking.

Career

At Leila Restaurant, Roy manages 20 employees. His ideal employee possesses awareness and presence. He believes a good manager should possess leadership qualities. His experience in motivating people and helping them see the value of the role they play are what make him a good manager. His specific management style includes inspiring and continually educating his staff. Something unique he does is consider his employees his most valuable asset.

The toughest lesson Roy learned was that it is just not that easy. The one thing he wished he had been told when he started in management was to have plenty of cash on the side. The best piece of advice that he was given was to find quality people and then hold on to them.

Leila's won many awards its first year in business and turned a profit the second year. In the next five to ten years, Roy wants to make sure they expand to the next level and create a restaurant that can be duplicated.

Roy was named one of 55 Most Fascinating People in Palm Beach County by Palm Beach Illustrated and was also named one of the most powerful people by South Florida CEO.

A change that they implemented at Leila's was changing the management and it coming out successfully. They are currently in the process of changing their head chef.

Leila's 2006 estimated sales were $1.4 million.

A Little Restaurant Information

Leila Restaurant serves Middle Eastern cuisine. They are members of their local Chamber of Commerce, as well as many other local organizations. They are open for lunch from 11:30 a.m. till 2:30 p.m. and dinner from 5:30 p.m. to 11 p.m. every day. Their busiest hour starts at 7 p.m., and they accept reservations. They do not require bouncers nor do they have valet parking. They serve beer and wine, but Roy does not believe alcohol is an important aspect to the business.

The ambiance, cuisine, and culture are what sets Leila's apart and draws in its clientele. In the evenings they have a belly dancer performance. They occasionally will cater.

All the food at the restaurant arrives fresh, and they do purchase some of it from local vendors. Roy describes the cuisine as fresh and healthy. His markup is three times. He says he has never had to adjust prices because of competition, but has found the best way to keep costs down is to be present often.

When a customer is unsatisfied with the service, food, or atmosphere of Leila Restaurant, Roy will comp their meal with no questions asked. There is not really a specific age group that prefers the restaurant. Frequent diners are recognized, but they do not offer any coupons in their advertising. Customer checks do not include gratuity.

When it comes to his wait staff, the most important trait Roy looks for is cleanliness and a great attitude. Roy has had to help his wait staff before, but has never had to step in for a chef. They do have a host/hostess and to some degree that staff member does have certain managerial duties over other employees. The staff is required to follow a dress code, but they do not require the men to wear ties. Roy does not use flex scheduling. To handle staff arguments Roy works on preventing them from even happening. The chef is responsible for evaluating the kitchen staff, and the wait staff is evaluated through a system that measures attendance, timeliness, and results.

Roy uses a computer to keep up with the daily records of Leila Restaurant. He contracts many outside professional services. The kitchen has all the equipment needed, and dishes are cleaned by machine. To reduce accidents they have instituted many maintenance measures.

Roy believes Leila Restaurant has reached his goal of what he wanted it to be, and when asked if he would do this all over again if he had the chance he said, "For sure, over and over."

Advice Tidbits

"Everyone in the organization must be respected and appreciated, from the dishwasher to the executive chef; if that is the culture, people stay."

Paul Barthel

Company	Peppercorns Restaurant
Address	877 Geneva Road
	Carol Steem, IL 60188
Role in Company	Chef / Owner
E-mail	paulbarthel@comcast.net
Web site	**peppercornsrestaurant.org**
Phone	630-871-7636
	708-715-3927 (Cell)
Fax	630-690-2969

A restaurant in Italy; Paul is on the left.

Background

Paul Barthel has been in the restaurant industry for 25 years and in management for 19 of those years. He has worked, by choice, in a variety of restaurants, including hotel and larger hospitality entertainment venues (Soldier Field and a race course facility). He decided to go into management for the employment.

"Currently I am the owner of a 130-seat family restaurant and am in the process of scouting for our second location. I began working in the business as a cook just to earn money. I managed to stay in business by working in many different departments. It was not until about eight years after getting into the business that I went to culinary school. Since then, I have worked in many restaurants until finally going into banquets where preparing food became more about volume. This became boring as well, until I then went into larger venue entertainment properties: Soldier Field, 2003 U.S. Open, Balmoral Park Race Course, and Navy Pier. My largest plate was 5,000 respectively and 10,000 buffet-style. I eventually had to address the "bug" in me to operate my own property, which is when I finally purchased my own restaurant."

Career

Paul Barthel now owns Peppercorns Restaurant, where he manages 25 employees. He says his ideal employee is friendly and has the ability to work well with others.

He believes a good manager is a person who has the ability to multitask with ease, can work well with others, and is people friendly. He says the quality he possesses that helps in his management career is the fact that he started working from the back of the house to the front and he has performed all the skills in the field. If a chef called in, he would be able to step in and cover the shift. He has a specific management style.

"I let people do their job, and most times will only interfere if they lose perspective of their job or the goal of the company. I do not micromanage. I believe in letting my employees know that they are the ones in control of their employment growth within the company, based on their performance."

Paul does a few unique things when it comes to managing his employees. He tends to be flexible in quality leave time and will often cover an employee's shift if they need the time off. He will also do the work he asks of his employees to show them that they are all in it together.

The toughest lesson Paul had to learn when he first started in management was that he needed others to make it happen.

"I tend to get things done on my own, yet in this field you will need others to carry your ideas from start to the customer's table."

When he first started in management, he wishes someone had told him not to go into the field. The best advice he was given was to get ready to work long hours.

Paul's goals for the next five or ten years are to operate their third restaurant and to finally get the book he has been working on published. So far in his career he has accumulated chef awards and appeared in many different periodicals. He enjoys working larger events like the 2003 U.S. Open in the corporate chef position and the inaugural season for the new Chicago Bears stadium. He is also very proud of opening his own restaurant.

In his career Paul completely changed the concept of his restaurant once he found out the original concept was not working. Those changes have been successful, and they have actually expanded on his ideas. A change he still would like to implement is to enlarge the bar area of the restaurant and increase their liquor revenues.

A Little Restaurant Information

Peppercorns Restaurant is a family restaurant that serves breakfast, lunch, and dinner. They also cater. The hours are from 6 a.m. to 9 p.m. Their busiest hours are Friday nights, all day Saturday, and Sunday breakfast.

"Dinner is somewhat more upscale by my choice since I need that creativity."

Alcohol is served at Peppercorns, and Paul says it is very important to the business. They are actually in the process of expanding their wine list and pushing alcohol through other means, such as wine tastings, Web site promotions, and table tents.

Peppercorns carries a few gift items, and sometimes they also have entertainment. They are also very creative with their food, which Paul believes sets the restaurant apart and draws in their clientele.

"The area that we are in tends to be populated with restaurants having dummied down menus that carry items that are simple to prepare. This means you do not have to employ a chef, and you can save that revenue. Yet you will lose the creativity since your kitchen employees lack the training or experience to prepare those items."

Paul believes the recent trend toward coffee shops has not affected his coffee sales negatively; rather it has increased them and drove his margins up to the point where they now have an espresso machine. He has found that colors affect appetite.

"We went to more earth tones in our restaurant. For example, we print our breakfast special card on yellow card stock paper to create a happy "wake up" attitude, while our evening cards are more subtle."

Paul is a member of his local Chamber of Commerce.

"Although I am a member I do not find it very useful to pay a premium and get together once a month over coffee with other business owners who only talk about the weather. My time is too valuable."

When it comes to their American casual cuisine, about 25 percent of the food arrives frozen and 75 percent arrives fresh. They usually have a nice turnover of items that do not require freezer space. They actually have a walk-in cooler but no freezer. Every week the fresh food is bought locally, especially the vegetables.

"I try to have an advantage over other local restaurants that carry frozen foods. I also convey to my customers that they are eating fresh, not frozen, foods."

Paul says he always adjusts his prices due to competition. He actually keeps a copy of all the area's menus, which keeps him at his best and encourages competition. His markup differs. He tries to keep the food costs at 30 percent, but when they run specials or promotions it will cost more toward 50 percent. He knows these specials will help retain a customer and that person will bring others along with them. To keep costs down he tries to maintain a good food cost, watches his labor, and checks his margins.

"If servers want to go home and it's slow, let them go home. If you're wasting or burning a lot of food, correct your chef. As a manager you have this responsibility every day, which will contribute to the bottom line at the end of the month."

When it comes to his staff, Paul looks for friendly, customer-oriented individuals. He looks for a server that can smile and is friendly, and says he can teach them all the rest. He has had to step in for his staff before, and he actually encourages it because it shows how willing he is to perform side-by-side with this staff. They have a host or hostess on all shifts.

"It all starts at the door when a customer walks in."

The host/ hostess does have managerial duties. They clean menus, work the floor, and make sure all the customers are attended to. Paul encourages them to interact with the customers.

"People love to talk about themselves and will actually come back if you show interest. Today it's not just about the food and pictures on the wall."

Paul is tolerant of flex scheduling because he knows he needs to have the best employees he can. His kitchen staff is evaluated by cleanliness and the quality of their food.

"If the kitchen is dirty it's a sign of no respect for their environment. You work and live in that kitchen every day. Would you want it to be dirty and unorganized?"

The wait staff is evaluated by their friendliness and speed and if the customer is happy.

"Did you meet all their needs? Don't worry about me, the owner; if your customers are happy and you keep a nice clean work space, I will never interfere with your work."

There is a uniform policy required for the staff, but the men do not have to wear ties.

Paul handles staff squabbles by finding out first what the problem is and then, if necessary, keeping those staff members on separate shifts if they cannot work out their issues.

Reservations are taken at Peppercorns. They just started taking reservations on their Web site as well. Paul encourages this for any type of restaurant or type of menu as he says it makes the guest feel more special and at the same time will let you know when a large party is coming in. They do not have valet parking nor do they require bouncers at the restaurant. Customer checks do not include gratuity.

Peppercorns has a mixed age group that seems to prefer the restaurant. In the beginning they had more seniors, but once menu changes and the inclusion of alcohol happened, they were able to expand their clientele. When it comes to a customer who is unhappy with the service, food, or atmosphere, Paul says this happens when they first walk in the door.

"In customer service you should be able to "read" a person at that point. And it is almost always at that point you know this person will need more "special" attention if he or she is having a bad day. By the time they are through and walking out the door, they should have forgotten their problems, at least for that period they were your guest."

They do reward frequent diners through the frequent diner program they have implemented. Although the program expired at one point, they did bring it back due to its high demand. Paul says it works and it creates high return business. He also offers coupons in his advertising.

"This encourages people to try your place that may have not known about it, and also can increase repeat dining."

Peppercorns uses a computer to keep their daily records as it is more professional and gives much more information for them to be able to compare and see what is and what is not working. Outside companies are hired for accounting, knife sharpening, and maintenance.

"I have an accountant since I do not have the time or expertise to fully utilize

the advantages of this field, a knife company simply because the knives are always sharp and fresh, and a maintenance program for all those equipment pieces that break down."

Dishes are washed through a machine. Right now, they have a low-temperature machine that uses chemicals to clean and sanitize, but Paul does not really care for it. He prefers a high-temperature machine that uses chemicals, but with the higher temperature it gets the dishes much cleaner. To reduce accidents in the restaurant, Paul does mopping only at designated times to avoid slips, he performs a lot of the tasks himself, and always has a second person around when performing those harder tasks.

When asked if Peppercorns had reached his dream of what he thought it should be, Paul said not yet.

"Rich Melman is a great role model and I would love to someday build an empire that he has achieved."

When asked if he would do all of it over again if he had to, Paul said he would have purchased his own restaurant years ago and not have waited as long.

"I did, however, learn many mistakes of the business and what not to do by watching others' failures."

Advice Tidbits

"Work in the field first before going to a hospitality school. Find out if you actually like it. Every day is a new day. It doesn't matter if yesterday you successfully fed 500 people in a plated sit down at $100 a plate, because tomorrow is another day and that party of five having waffles in your restaurant deserve just as much attention and could care less what you did yesterday."

Heather Chell

Company	Avenue Diner
Address	105, 8th Avenue SW
	Calgary, AB T2P 1B4
	Canada
Role in Company	GM / Proprietor
E-mail	info@avenuediner.com
Web site	**www.avenuediner.com**
Phone	403-263-2673
Fax	403-266-2674

AVENUE DINER

Background

Heather Chell has been in the restaurant industry for 15 years. She has been in management for approximately nine years of that time so far. Besides Avenue Diner, she also worked for many other fine dining establishments. Her first job in the hospitality field was as a server. Heather decided to become a restaurant manager because she felt a real pull to contribute.

"I love a challenge, and I'd almost always rather be working on or in a restaurant than doing anything else."

Born into a food family, Heather has the natural ability to recognize that food both nurtures the soul and fills the belly.

"One of my earliest memories of childhood is sitting on the counter with my mom and grandma who were patiently showing me how to properly pinch the edges of a pierogi. They had an assembly line going, but when I landed more food on the floor than onto their sheet pans, they moved me to "mixing duty," where my job was to combine all the mashed potatoes and Cheddar together in a big green bowl with my hands. I just loved it! I was about four at the time."

The concept that food has the power to nurture and bring people together has been a running theme throughout Heather's life. As she watched and helped her grandmother, mother, and aunts prepare dinner in the weeks leading up to Christmas, Heather began to understand that all this was about more than the meal itself; it had become an important ritual that would bring the women (and on occasion the men) in her family together, to focus solely on one another.

"It was the most beautiful, fulfilling feeling…everyone coming together under one roof to put this amazing meal together in order to make our family and friends feel cared for and loved. It was that feeling that hooked me like a drug. I had completely fallen in love with the nurturing powers of food and I wanted to base my life on it. It was inevitable."

Heather received her formal training at Dubrulle French Culinary School in Vancouver, British Columbia, where she graduated at the top of her class and landed the desirable position of class valedictorian. Prior to that, she studied Food Sciences through Athabasca University in Alberta via correspondence while living abroad and working in the restaurant industry. Over the past ten years, Heather has worked in, cooked at, managed, consulted for, owned, and operated a slew of different restaurants and event companies in various parts of the world. Her pursuit of excellence has taken her from Grand Cayman to southern California to Toronto and back up to Calgary, Alberta, Canada, where she is most currently immersed in her latest project — a 70 seat urban diner and catering company specializing in "gourmet comfort food" and progressive, class-A catered fare. The restaurant recently won a category in Where Magazine's "Most Memorable Meal Awards," which was released in January of 2007. Additionally, Heather's creative eats and recognition as one of Calgary's up and coming food entrepreneurs has been picked up by a local television station, which began running a live, monthly cooking segment a few years ago.

"Once I realized I could combine the culinary arts with the notion of making people happy through excellence in food, wine, and service, my life started down a very different, very unplanned, and beautiful path. I never really had any preconceived idea of what my life in the business would look like, but because it was innate in me, my career as a hospitality industry professional just seemed to unfold naturally. There's nothing else I'd rather be doing."

Heather currently resides in Calgary with her two chocolate labs, Hunter and Kaizen, who are always enthusiastic about clean up time in the kitchen.

Career

Heather now owns her own restaurant, Avenue Diner where she manages 20 employees. She says her ideal employee possesses the following qualities: pride, a sense of responsibility, dedication to growth, diligence, and perseverance.

She believes some of the qualities she possesses that help her in her management career are having a true passion for excellence, being humble, independent, creative, and having a strong sense of courage. She believes it takes many things to be a good manager.

"A genuine desire to get to know your employees, knowing how to build cohesive teams, giving rewards and recognition, commitment to training/cross-training, setting the tone everyday, ability to set deadlines and prioritize, goal setting, ability to take responsibility for the details, create challenges for employees, empower staff to make decisions on their own, and employment of compassion."

Heather says one thing she does that is unique when managing is that she listens – really listens. Her specific management style includes being independent and influential.

"I am comfortable taking charge without abusing my power. Additionally, I try to embrace a real "in the trenches" approach while motivating each employee to reach the top through learning and understanding what makes each person feel important in their own unique way. I am also open to new ways of thinking."

The toughest lesson and the one piece of advice she wishes she had been given when she first started in restaurant management was that, even in the most critical times (for example, a nationwide labor shortage), to never, ever excuse inexcusable behavior.

"Under performance is toxic."

The best piece of advice she was given when she started was that absentee ownership is one of the biggest contributing factors to all restaurant failures. She was also told to never be afraid or too proud to ask questions. Heather has done one major thing thus far in her management career that she has been proud of accomplishing:

"I introduced the gourmet, high-end diner concept to the city and pioneered the idea of demanding quality ingredients prepared by talented and skilled professionals for more than just lunch and dinner."

A change Heather would like to implement is some sort of performance-based incentive program for the front house and kitchen manager.

"The purpose would be to keep them engaged and to create a symbiotic, win-win situation for both myself and for my key players."

Heather works with the community as well.

"I am a mentor for the Hera Society, an organization for adolescent girls at risk."

A Little Restaurant Information

Avenue Diner serves gourmet comfort food, old favorites with unique, epicurean spins. They are open for breakfast, lunch, and brunch.

"Avenue Diner offers natural foods…healthy, seasonal, and organic whenever possible. We use the best and freshest ingredients available. Menu offerings are

full of everything from organic, fairly traded coffee to our delicious waffles made with blood orange butter and wild blueberries, apple smoked bacon and double cream Brie-stuffed Brioche toast to locally raised bison burgers topped with double smoked bacon, vintage Cheddar, and chipotle mayo. All this is located in one beautifully designed space complete with the original sandstone brick wall from the building's inception way back in 1898. A seamless blend of history and urban chic lends a hand in creating an unforgettable dining experience in the heart of downtown Calgary."

The busiest times for the restaurant are breakfast, lunch, and weekend brunch. They do serve alcohol, and it is important to the business. Heather finds that colors affect a customer's appetite. Avenue Diner does offer selective catering. They do not take reservations, do not have valet parking, and do not require bouncers. The checks do not include gratuity. The age group that seems to prefer Avenue Diner is 25 to 50 year olds. The fact that they make everything from scratch and most of the menu is comprised of locally sourced ingredients is what Heather believes sets Avenue Diner apart and draws in clientele. They also use organic, locally roasted beans for their coffee, and Heather says people love it.

Regular customers at Avenue Diner receive special treatment for frequent dining. They do not offer coupons in advertising.

"I believe if you have to discount your product in order to attract new guests, there's a bigger problem at hand that needs to be addressed."

When a customer has a complaint, it is always handled with "kid gloves." They take the concerns of their customers very seriously and have a manager on duty (MOD) at all times to deal with any possible issues that may arise.

"The MOD would speak directly with guests to gain a good understanding of how we could ensure the guest left feeling cared for and satisfied. Whether it means firing up an alternative from the kitchen, taking care of a dry cleaning bill for a spill, or even driving a guest to their destination if service time kept them tardy for an appointment — we stop at nothing to provide the best possible experience we can. We also log any complaints in our daily log, which would then be discussed on Monday morning at our weekly management meeting."

Heather buys the fresh food used at Avenue Diner locally and 100 percent of the foods used are fresh. They have never adjusted prices to compete.

"We're good, and our pricing is very, very fair, especially for the quality of ingredients and level of service offered."

The most important trait that Heather looks for in wait staff is to have an innate desire to truly delight guests. She does have a dress code for her wait staff. Uniforms are simply dark denim jeans, black long-or short-sleeved shirts, and comfortable black shoes. The men are not required to wear ties.

The MOD or Heather herself acts as host/ hostess. Heather has had to step in for all positions in the restaurant at one time or another.

"I have been in front house operations throughout my entire career; however, I am also professionally trained through a renowned French Culinary academy.

Additionally, I have been known to jump into the dish pit on more than one occasion. If I am needed —I am available."

Heather does allow flex schedules for herself, her bookkeeper, and sometimes for her manager. The kitchen and wait staffs are evaluated by performance reviews after each quarter. To handle staff squabbles, Heather goes right to the source(s) of the problem.

A computer is used to keep daily records for the restaurant. They outsource linen service, knife sharpening, cleaning, some baking (not all), and menu and stationery printing. The kitchen has all the equipment needed. To wash the dishes, hands, machines, sanitizers, and heat are all used. Two of the many things Avenue Diner has done to prevent accidents are placing mats out front during the winter and making sure food safety is followed closely in the kitchen and out front areas.

When Heather was asked if Avenue Diner has fulfilled her dream of what it should be she said this:

"The answer is yes, although that's a tough question to answer. Regardless of our success, I make a point of staying aware of our shortcomings and never resting on our laurels. Things don't always pan out exactly the way I envision them, but in the big picture, I am very happy with the results and am extremely grateful for the entire experience."

If she had to do it all over again, Heather said she absolutely would!

Advice Tidbits

"Think big because there's always room at the top!"

Paul & Linda Joerger

Company	Altitudes Bar & Grill
Address	Two S. Beaver, Suite 2
	Flagstaff, AZ 86001
Role in Company	Owners
	Paul — General Manager
	Lynda — Manager / Marketing
E-mail	paulyndaj@infomagic.com
Phone	928-214-8218
Fax	928-773-0414

Background

Paul Joerger has been in the restaurant industry for 25 years and in management for 15. Lynda Fleischer-Joerger has been in the restaurant industry for 30 years and in management for 10. They both became restaurant managers because they feel the restaurant business is fun and rewarding as well as lucrative.

Career

Paul Joerger and Lynda Fleischer-Joerger own Altitudes Bar & Grill, where they manage 18 employees, including two front-of-house supervisors and one kitchen supervisor. Their ideal employee is professional, caring, responsible, outgoing, and honest. They believe that all those qualities, as well as an understanding of people, are also needed to be a good manager. They care about their staff and let them have a share of their success. Their management style is very open, and they also offer occasional incentives.

The toughest lesson they have learned so far in their management careers, and the piece of advice they wish they had been given when they first started was to not trust anyone. Their goal is to open another restaurant in the next five or ten years. They are very proud that Altitudes received the Small Business Success Award 2006. A change they implemented was tipping out the back of the house from the front of the house. They wanted to reward their kitchen staff for working harder when the restaurant is busy. It has been a very positive change for them.

A Little Restaurant Information

Altitudes Bar & Grill serves American food, such as burgers, salads, soups, chili, wraps, barbeque, appetizers, and entrees. They also do catering and accept reservations. Their hours of operation are from 11:30 a.m. to midnight. They serve food daily until 10 p.m., and closing time depends on the crowd, but is usually not past midnight. Their busiest hours are from noon to 1 p.m. and from 6:30 to 7:30 p.m.

They do serve alcohol, and it is an important part of their business. Some things that set apart their restaurant are its ski theme, being locally owned, its train shots, great food and service, and location. They also offer television and musicians. They do not require bouncers and do not have valet parking.

They buy their fresh foods locally and are members of the Southside Business Alliance and their local Chamber of Commerce. They say they have never had to adjust their pricing due to their competition and say the management is the best way to keep their costs down. There is not really an age group that prefers the restaurant more than another.

Paul and Lynda deal with unsatisfied customers differently depending on each situation. They offer discounts to skiers/snowboarders and Chamber of Commerce members, offer coupons that support the Special Olympics, work with a local insurance agent to offer complimentary lunch to his clients, and occasionally hand out appetizer coupons to hotels and travelers. Their customer checks do not include gratuity.

The most important trait Paul and Lynda look for in their wait staff is honesty. They do have to step in for members of their staff sometimes. They do not have a host or hostess. Their staff members are required to follow a dress code, which includes casual pants, skirts, or shorts with an Altitude's logo shirt. The men are not required to wear ties. They do not use flex scheduling for their employees. When they have trouble with staff arguments they handle it up front.

Outside contractors provide linen service, grease trap removal, and maintenance services. Bathrooms are cleaned by an outside source, and a computer is used to keep the daily records of the restaurant. They have most of the kitchen equipment needed, but they do have to do a little make-do. Dishes are washed by machines.

Paul and Lynda say Altitudes has reached the dream of what they thought it would be, and if they had to do it all over again they would.

Jay Johnson

Company	Bubba's Roadhouse & Saloon
Address	2121 SW Pine Island Road Cape Coral, FL 33991
Role in Company	Owner
E-mail	bubbasroadhouse@excite.com
Web site	**www.bubbasroadhouse.net**
Phone	239-282-5520
Fax	239-282-5523

Background

Jay Johnson has been in the restaurant industry for 27 years and in management for 20 of those years. Besides Bubba's Roadhouse & Saloon,

Jay has also worked at Brown Derby, McDonald's, and Sheraton Hotels. His first job in the hospitality field was as a dishwasher at Brown Derby in Cleveland, Ohio. He decided to become a restaurant manager because it was a family tradition. He graduated from the University of Denver with a major in Hotel and Restaurant Management. He worked for ITT Sheraton in Hawaii, Seattle, Miami, Orlando, Chicago, Los Angeles, and Tucson. He left being the hotel manager at Sheraton to move to Florida and start his own business.

Career

Jay now owns his own restaurant, Bubba's Roadhouse & Saloon, where he manages 50 employees. He says the qualities his ideal employee possesses are a willingness to please the customer, quick thinking, a willingness to work hard, and a nice personality.

He believes it takes many things to be a good manager, including a firmness while being fair, an ability to adjust to any situation, an understanding of accounting and how every area of business interacts with each other (marketing, human resources, and finance), and being able to treat people as individuals, knowing that what works with one person may not work with another.

Understanding and the ability to adapt to each situation are the qualities he possesses that help him in his management career. His specific management style is to be very open and honest. He treats his employees as he would like to be treated himself.

The toughest lesson Jay has learned in management has been to approach each situation with an open mind. When he first started in management he wishes he had been told to treat his employees right because they would take care of him, and to take time for himself. The best piece of advice he was given when first starting was to listen to his employees.

Jay's goal for the next few years is to continue to build the business. His estimated 2006 sales were $2 million. Something he is very proud of is that Bubba's Roadhouse & Saloon hosted President Carter and his family for dinner in 2005.

A Little Restaurant Information

Bubba's Roadhouse & Saloon is a steakhouse that serves hand-cut steaks, barbeque ribs, chicken, and seafood. The restaurant is open from 11:30

a.m. to 11 p.m., and their busiest hour is 5 p.m. They do accept reservations but do not offer valet parking. Alcohol is served and is considered an important aspect to the business. They also do catering. Jay says being a local roadhouse with fresh food and drink sets them apart and draws in their clientele. They also have live music on Friday and Saturday nights. They are a member of their local Chamber of Commerce.

The age group that seems to prefer Bubba's Roadhouse & Saloon is the 40 and up group. Customer checks do not include gratuity. They do not reward their frequent diners nor do they offer coupons in their advertising.

About 5 percent of the foods arriving at Bubba's are frozen and 95 percent arrives fresh. They do not buy their fresh foods locally. Jay says they have never had to adjust their pricing due to their competition and that the best way to keep costs down is to order smart and keep waste to a minimum.

The most important traits Jay looks for in his wait staff are a good smile and friendliness. He has had to step in for members of his staff before. They do have a host/hostess, but they do not have managerial duties over the other staff members. They do not require bouncers. The staff does have to follow a dress code of a Bubba's Roadhouse & Saloon shirt, jeans, and black non-slip shoes, but the men are not required to wear ties. He does use flex scheduling. He evaluates his wait staff by their demeanor with the guests and fellow co-workers, knowledge of the menu, and sales ability.

Outside companies are hired to wash the towels and sharpen the knives for the restaurant. A computer is used to keep the daily records. The kitchen has all the equipment needed and no make-do is required. A machine is used to wash the dishes. To reduce accidents in the restaurant, all staff members are required to wear non-slip shoes.

When asked if he had to do it all over again, Jay responded he would "in a heartbeat."

Ron Kalenuik

Company	Kalenuik Food Services, Inc.
Address	240 Wade Ave. W. Penticton, BC, Canada, V2A-1T8
Role in Company	President
E-mail	chefk@chefk.com
Web site	**www.chefk.com**
Phone	250.492-7383
Fax	250-493-4815

Background

Ron Kalenuik, affectionately known as Chef K (by those who could not pronounce his last name) began his culinary career in the Rocky Mountains of Alberta, Canada in 1974. Since then he went on to establish himself as an award-winning Chef de Cuisine in many fine restaurants in North America before he owned and operated several national, award-winning restaurants of his own. He is a teacher and consultant to the hospitality industry, as well as a television host and author of 18 different cookery books to date, which have been released in as many as 19 languages and sold in 64 countries worldwide.

His international bestsellers include *Simply Delicious Cooking* and *Simply Delicious Cooking 2*, which have sold more than 2.5 million copies. Other titles by Chef K include *International Family Favourites*, *The Original Pizza & Pasta Book*, *Fundamentals of Taste*, *Cuisine Extraordinaire*, *Fresh Ideas*, *The Right Spice*, and *Championship Cooking*.

Chef K hosts television's *Divine Cuisine*, which has been broadcast on 140 stations and 5 satellite networks. Locally, he hosts the *Jazz Café* radio program heard Sunday's at 10:00 a.m. and midnight on The Giant FM (100.7 FM).

Career

Ron Kalenuik, aka Chef K, has been in the restaurant industry for 30 years and in management for 25 of those years. Besides his current restaurant, he also worked for fast food places, as well as some causal and fine dining establishments. His first job in the hospitality industry was as a waiter. He decided to go into management after being pressured by the restaurant chain he was working for at that time.

At Chef K's Restaurant he manages up to 150 employees. His ideal employee is capable of providing good and friendly service with knowledge of the services that are offered, as well as having the desire to learn beyond the job description.

Chef K believes that a good restaurant manager needs the ability to lead by example, life style, belief, and education (both life and formal), as well as being able to work well under pressure and remain calm and in control. He says the quality that he possesses that helps in his management career is creativity.

"The creative person will show the ability to take a problem and, through the creative process, formulate and implement the required solutions. The creative person will view their position as an exciting challenge and not a chore; once a position becomes a chore it becomes a job and no longer a career. Creativity keeps the person motivated and interested in doing better."

Chef K considers himself more of a mentor than manager, as he prefers to give those who work with him an opportunity to learn. He tries to provide an avenue where he can lead by example and motivate through creativity, which he believes allows for constructive communication and fulfilling of the vision of his operation. Something he does that is unique to his management style is being there for his employees during the good and rough times.

"The restaurateur is motivated by an attitude of 'how can I serve you,' but that is not just for their patron; it must be for the staff as well. The staff wants to be treated as equals, and while the job is service, the life of serving can be quite a difference. Hospitality is defined as the reception and entertainment of guests or strangers with liberality and kindness. Staff members are guests invited into your business to ensure its success and so should be treated as such (as defined above). From the Latin word hospitare meaning 'to receive as a guest' and in Greek 'the love of strangers.' The best way to describe hospitality is 'one is motivated by compassion.' Of course, compassion is not just a feeling of sympathy, it is 'to experience what another undergoes and have the power to change it.' What every food service establishment does minute by minute with their patrons, this too should be what every leader does with their associates."

Chef K says the toughest lesson he has learned in his management career has been when financial losses occur because of avoidable mistakes. He sees losses as a failure to win the trust of patrons and/or staff, which is what he believes creates a successful establishment.

"When we make mistakes that are clearly avoidable it speaks to our lack of trust

in ourselves and our abilities. We will suffer loses, but we must do everything possible to make them as small as possible. Making our decisions based on as many sound factors as possible. When we knowingly do that which is contrary to sound business and service, we set ourselves up for a loss."

The best piece of advice Chek K received when he first started in management was to "do what's right, do it because it is right, then do it right." He believes that if managers would implement that thinking into their everyday service their success would be ensured.

"You cannot fail when you're doing what is right. Don't cut corners, don't go cheap, don't cheat, don't lie, et cetera. We all seem to know these things, yet we see them done daily in our business. Menus that promise one thing but deliver something else, managers instructing servers to make claims in food descriptions that are not true, and so much more. If we will just follow the simple principal of doing what's right, doing it because it is right, then doing it right, we will live well with ourselves and with others."

Chef K was once given the opportunity to create a continuing education program for the hard to employ or new immigrants. After he created it and taught the course, the program was actually placed in the public school education program in which many students were able to choose the hospitality industry as their career. This is something in his career that he has been acknowledged for. He has also done many other things in his career so far that he is proud of.

"I have written a total of 23 cookbooks, 18 of which have been published. The bestselling ones have been translated into 19 languages and released in 64 countries; one, Simply Delicious Cooking 2 (an 800 page book), is used as a text in many cooking schools. This makes me feel good that young people continue to seek to become good cooks."

When asked about what kind of changes he has implemented or would like to implement, he had this to say:

"Major changes come from a series of minor ones; make the changes that are required as they come and a major one may not be required. An innovated, motivated operator will stay on top of what changes are coming and will reflect those changes in service, food, and atmosphere."

In the next five years, Chef K would like to see a continued growth in his business.

"We presently are working with a developer who will be building a series of different food service establishments and our job is to ensure the success of each. We would like to continue to do this for other companies as well (whether they are large or small, corporate or independent)."

A Little Restaurant Information

Chef K's Restaurant is open from 11:30 a.m. to 2:00 p.m. for lunch and 5:00 p.m. to 11:00 p.m. for dinner. From noon to 1:00 p.m. is their busiest hour. The cuisine served at the restaurant is South Eastern with Cajun and Creole features. Alcohol is served and is important to the business. They offer live jazz on the weekends. They do offer catering for parties of 50 or more. They do not yet offer valet parking, and do not have a need for bouncers, but they do accept reservations. Although they were a member of their local Chamber of Commerce in the past, they are not presently. The age group that seems to prefer the restaurant is 30 to 65 year olds. Chef K says the care and attention to the patrons in all details are what sets his restaurant apart and draws in customers.

Chef K rewards his frequent diners in many ways (such as complementary dinners or drinks, magic nights, supporting of local fund raising, and pink drink night for the ladies), but does not offer any coupons in advertising. When he has a customer who is not happy with the food, service, or atmosphere, he says he must consider the complaint as a gift, as that means someone is truly concerned about the food or service.

"We have been given a valuable tool to make a change to better what we do. In today's world, the patron looks for not just good service but that which is superior; they look for the WOW experience (we offer wonderful). An unhappy customer is a walking time bomb on your business. One study once showed a happy customer talked about the restaurant to about 30 people, whereas an unhappy one talked to about 200. Food and service has one simple rule: Make it right for them NOW. Décor is different; I can only recall one complaint on décor, which was a lady who could not do her makeup to match the décor and therefore she would not return. What can you do with that?"

Chef K describes the cuisine at the restaurant as casual dining. He uses 12 percent frozen foods and 88 percent fresh foods. He buys as much of the fresh food as possible from local vendors. He has not had trouble with the recent trend toward coffee shops and says this is because of their own blend.

"We blend our coffee ourselves using four different beans; it is very good and well received. I would recommend every restaurant develop a signature blend of coffee, especially if they are losing a share of their business to the upscale coffee vendors."

When it comes to his employees, Chef K does use flex scheduling. There is a host/hostess as well, but they do not have any managerial duties over the other employees. He does require a dress code for the staff (black shirts and pants with a long white server's apron), but the men are not required to wear ties. The most important trait he looks for in his wait staff is how knowledgeable and eager they are to learn.

"A teachable person is a valuable asset to any business."

When the staff squabbles, Chef K usually tries first a simple one-on-one conversation to resolve the problem depending on what it is. If the problem is more serious, a harsher method may be required to resolve it. He has had to step in for members of his staff before.

"You cannot lead by example if you cannot perform the same duties you are requesting of your associates."

The following four-point system is used to evaluate his staff:

A) Has the employee implemented the skills for which they have been hired or have been taught?

B) What is the performance objective of the employee and have they met it?

C) Through observation, has the manager observed the employee in all the job functions, and if so, what is the manager's opinion of the employee's performance?

D) Has the employee or manager made any assumption regarding their performance; are the assumptions fact or fiction?

A computer is used to keep the daily records of the restaurant, and some outside companies are hired to do some of the jobs that require professionals, such as federal government reporting and accounting, heavy soil cleaning, staff uniform laundry, and, of course, the musicians required to give the customer a great dining experience. Outside companies are only hired if they can do the job better and save the restaurant money.

The dishes at the restaurant are cleaned by machine with chemical and high temperature water. Although most of the kitchen equipment is make-do, Chef K says this allows for creative thinking and problem solving. One of the best steps he has instituted to reduce accidents in the restaurant is education.

"The more of your staff with First Aid and CPR training, the more likely accidents won't happen. Pay for the staff to take the training, and it will pay back to you in less accidents and possible lives saved. I personally have had to use life saving methods three times over my 30 years for customers. In addition be sure to provide what is required for the employee to perform in a safe manner."

Chef K has never had to adjust his pricing because of competition. Large group checks do include gratuity. He has found the best way to keep costs down is by watching them.

"Restaurants do not make dollars per plate; they make pennies, and therefore the best way to make the pennies is to watch where every one is spent. Control

the things that can be controlled and the profit will take care of itself."

Chef K says the restaurant has not yet fulfilled his dream of what it should be, but he is working on it. When asked if he had it do all over again, he says he would "in a heartbeat."

Advice Tidbits

"Do what is right, do it because it is right, then do it right. Be wise in finding out what is right for your customer and never assume you know without performing what is required to find out for sure."

Kelly Keller

Company	BIN 239
Address	239 N. Marina St. Prescott, AZ 86301
Role in Company	Managing Partner
E-mail	winegeeks@bin239.com
Web site	**www.bin239.com**
Phone	928-445-3855
Fax	928-445-9264

Background

Kelly Keller has been in the restaurant industry for 35 years and in management for 28 of those years. Besides his current restaurant employment, Kelly worked for his family restaurant business, which was built in 1950 and is still family owned. He also was F&B Director and Divisional F&B Director for Hyatt Hotels and Starwood Hotels. His first job in the hospitality field was as a dishwasher. When asked why he decided to become a restaurant manager, Kelly said this:

"If one wants to move up the ladder in the industry, management is the way to get there. You go from working 40 hours a week to working 90 hours a week when you become a manager."

Career

Kelly now owns his own restaurant, BIN 239. When he was in the hotel and resort industry he managed approximately 600 employees, but with his own business he now manages 30 employees.

Kelly says honesty, integrity, credibility, and a personal goal in life are what qualities his ideal employee should possess. The ability to stay focused and having a thick skin are what he believes it takes to be a good manager.

Kelly says his ability to delegate is one quality that has helped in his management career. His specific management style includes listening before he reacts and never forgetting to say "thank you." Something he does that he believes is unique when it comes to managing his employees is his ability to sandwich constructive criticism with positive reinforcement.

One of the toughest lessons Kelly has learned while in his management career is that hard work is not always rewarded. When he first started in restaurant management the one thing he wishes he had been told was how tough management is.

Kelly's goal for the next five to ten years is to take his business to franchise.

He earned F&B Director of the Year company-wide in 1998. One of the things he is proud of in his career is the number of former managers and line staff that have kept in touch with him. Some changes he managed to implement in his career were during his time with Hyatt Hotels. These core wine list and food pairings are still in place today.

His current sales in his business are estimated at $1.5 million. When he was with Hyatt Hotels it was $110 million and with Starwood Hotels it was $53 million.

A Little Restaurant Information

BIN 239 is a café wine bar that serves wood-oven pizza, Panini sandwiches, salads, soups, and made in-house desserts. There is an extensive wine list and beer is offered as well since alcohol is a large component of the business. It is open from 11 a.m. to 10 p.m. daily, with lunch and dinner being its busiest periods. They do a little high-end catering as well. They do not take reservations and do not have valet parking. They are not a part of the local Chamber of Commerce.

Kelly says that having great people serve great people is something that sets BIN 239 apart from other restaurants and draws clientele in. They never let a guest leave unhappy.

When it comes to the food, Kelly says it is all fresh, but they do not buy it locally. He describes the cuisine offered as healthy, but flavorful. For coffee, they serve fresh-press.

Kelly has outside companies that do payroll and accounting for the restaurant. He uses a computer to keep track of daily records.

BIN 239 attracts mostly affluent 25 to 65 year old customers. He says they have never reduced prices due to competition. They do reward frequent diners with gift certificates, but do not offer coupons in advertising. Sometimes the checks include gratuity. He does believe that colors affect appetite.

The most important trait Kelly looks for in his wait staff is a genuine smile. He also works in the kitchen daily, redesigns the menu, and changes the food items on a continual basis. He does have hosts/hostesses who also have managerial duties over staff. He does have a uniform dress code for his wait staff that is provided. The dress code does not allow piercings, males with earrings, rainbow hair colors, and only one earring per ear and one standard color nail polish for females. The men are not required to wear ties. The restaurant does not require bouncers. He handles squabbles amongst the staff one on one.

They do flex scheduling for the employees. Because he is daily working side-by-side with his kitchen staff, Kelly is able to evaluate them every day. To evaluate his wait staff, he observes them while working. They have had no accidents in the restaurant.

Kelly's food markup for BIN 239 is dependant on the item, but he does use an X 21/2+8 for wines. The best way he has found to keep costs down is by being present at all times. He says the kitchen is like all kitchens out there in that there is always a need for more equipment. A machine does the dishes for the restaurant.

When asked if his restaurant had achieved his dream of what it should be, Kelly says he is never satisfied. If he had to do it all over again, he says he would.

Advice Tidbits

"Stay focused, arrive early, and leave late. Keep your friends close and your enemies closer. Use the 'Management by Walking Around' technique."

Nazir N. Khamisa

Company	San Delico, Inc.
Address	P.O. Box 477 Kirkland, WA 98083
Role in Company	President
E-mail	nazirk@comcast.net
Web site	**www.bin239.com**
Phone	206-227-7750
Fax	206-770-8925

Background

Nazir N. Khamisa has been in the restaurant industry for 19 years. He has been in management for 30 years and 19 of those are from restaurant management. He has opened, owned, and operated almost 20 restaurants in the last 19 years, and he decided to go into business for himself after managing hotels for other people for many years. His first job was actually in the hospitality field as manager of a full-service hotel. He attended college in England as well as at the University of Washington.

His family began purchasing hotels in Washington and Canada. Nazir and his wife, Shelina, began managing the hotels in Washington while he attended school, and eventually they partnered into a property investment that included a lounge, restaurant, and a banquet facility. There is where he learned food costs, inventory procedures, and operating a restaurant. He eventually leased the property out to a man who would then become partners with him in a steak and seafood restaurant that eventually branched into five chains. He expanded into many other restaurant businesses in Seattle when he and his wife returned after the birth of their daughter so they could be closer to their family. He also opened up a food court with five cuisine options. See the box below for all of Nazir's restaurants.

NAZIR'S THEN & NOW RESTAURANT EMPIRE		
Restaurant	# of Locations	# Locations Closed
Spice Restaurant & Lounge	1 — Seattle, WA	
Beba's Deli	11 — Bellevue & Seattle, WA	2
Dos Amigos	2 — Seattle, WA	
Claypit Grill and Curry House	1 — Dallas, TX	

NAZIR'S THEN & NOW RESTAURANT EMPIRE		
Chutney's	4 — Queen Anne, Capitol Hill, Wallingford, & Bellevue, WA	All 4 no longer owned by Nazir
Chin Chins Chinese Restaurant	1 — Seattle, WA	1 — Closed so Spice could open

Career

Nazir manages 25 employees at his restaurant. His ideal employee is professional, fun, friendly, honest, loyal, takes ownership, is a good team player, is well groomed, courteous, and respectful. He believes he possesses the qualities he thinks a good manager should have, which include being someone who can look at each team member for their individual strengths, who has a good eye for detail, loves people, and is passionate about the work he or she is doing. His specific management style includes creating a family type atmosphere in all of his establishments.

"This allows me to empower the team members because they care and take ownership due to the fact that they are as much a part of the success of the business as anybody else in the organization."

Something unique Nazir does when managing his employees is getting to know each one on an individual level, one-on-one.

"Each one is equally important to me as is given the same courtesy as any other—we are all a family."

The toughest lesson he has had to learn in his career thus far has been that his type of management style has its drawbacks.

"If you have somebody that is not inclined to embrace this culture then they can

take advantage of you and this can cause a different set of problems."

The advice Nazir wishes he was given when he first started in management was that there has to be boundaries, rules, and regulations set and they have to be respected and adhered to by everybody.

"Expectations should be made very clear, training should be very thorough, and there should be good follow up. When there is no follow up, there has to be accountability."

The best advice he was given was that he is running a business and the object of running a business is that it has to make money.

"In order to make money you must follow a code of ethics and adherence to running it in a professional manner with the end goal always in site."

Nazir's goal for the next five or ten years is to help people see the importance of running a business in a certain way in order to be able to reduce stress in management.

"This is a very tough business to be in — it has the highest mortality rate than any other business. It also has the highest burnout rate, hence the highest turnover rate for employees. I have employees that are still with me after 18 years; this reduces the stress level quite considerably. In the end you are only as good as the team you put together."

Nazir was given an award for Retail Person of the Year by the minority Business Association through the U.S. Chamber of Commerce. Most of the restaurants he has owned are now being run by his former employees as well as being owned by them. He is very proud of this.

"They were there for me and in turn I was able to help them become owners themselves."

Nazir's newest venture is Spice Restaurant and Lounge, which he opened to appeal to neighborhood of downtown Seattle and the entire city. They are open for lunch, happy hour, dinner, as well as a late-night scene. The food has a global flavor and spice. Part of the building was leased for the lounge section of Spice which serves global cocktails. The bar area offers over 20 plates that can be shared and the dining room area is for individual meals. Three chefs cook the diverse, international menu. The food ranges from Mediterranean to Thai to Spanish to burgers. Some of their dishes are vegetarian and each dish is authentic to whatever area it is from so there is not much fusion cooking.

"One of the things I have always wanted to get across to the public is that foods roasted in the clay oven are very healthy. All the fat is trimmed off, and the meat is marinated in a yogurt-based marinade. It goes into a 600-degree oven, so any fat left in the meat has no chance of survival. High heat has a unique ability to seal in the juices and the yogurt acts as a natural tenderizer. Plus, the meat never touches any surface like a char broiler. The result is a perfectly roasted tender and juicy piece of meat. Vegetables are blanched quickly, and then seared in a wok. Due to the high heat, it's a quick stir-fry, which leaves all the goodness of the vegetable intact, and juices are not lost. With the addition of world spice flavors in these foods, people will be enjoying great healthy food with amazing flavors."

Advice Tidbits

"Run your business in such a way that it is a franchised location especially if you are independent. Having rules, regulations, and systems in place is good for everybody as there is no question about what is expected."

I have been in business in one way or the other for the last 25 years. My stint in business has been all-encompassing, from washing dishes to being the CEO with over 200 employees under me; from taking over a business to opening businesses from scratch; from remodeling a business to actually taking a shell and building it from scratch; and from being a sole proprietor to having several partners. I personally am of the opinion that there are very few issues that I have not encountered in one way or another. I can honestly say that I went to the school of hard knocks and came out with a pretty decent GPA.

So what are some of the lessons I have learned? Many, and those I have listed here will be an attempt to archive some of the learning:

1) I have been guilty of being a slave to my business. I have been guilty of letting the business run me rather than me running the

business. People typically go into business for themselves because they have a passion for what they do and mainly to gain personal and financial freedom. The assumption is that this journey will be fun and fulfilling; also, why not? After all, I am in charge, I do not punch a time clock, I can create my own life style. Instead, I became a slave to my business.

2) Imagine a job that does not allow sick days, demands that you work overtime all the time, offers no paid vacations, makes you babysit employees, and then compensates you for an amount that basically pays pittance or sometimes is not even the equivalent of the least paid employee when you count the remuneration versus the number of hours you put into doing your job. How long would you stay? Would you believe me if I told you that the majority of the small business owners are in this boat?

3) Furthermore, statistics are not on our side as entrepreneurs. Did you know that very few businesses fail because of bankruptcy? Most fail because the owners come to the conclusion that the effort versus the return they receive is just not worth it. If you have dreams of growing and are able to make your business successful, did you know that only 1 in 600 businesses will ever grow to $10 million in revenues? Only 1 in 1,000 will grow to $50 million. Only 1 in 5 will actually sell. In fact, according to the U.S. Department of Commerce 96 percent of businesses will fail before their tenth birthday.

4) This is a scary statement, but most business owners would have a greater probability of success in Vegas.

   a) The standard approach to business gives you a 20 percent chance of success in the first five years.

b)   Slot machines have a 32 percent probability of success.

c)   Black Jack gives you a 45 percent probability of success.

d)   Roulette gives you a 47 percent probability of success.

Well, the university of hard knocks that I graduated from taught me what not to do. Thus, this will be an attempt to pass on some of this wisdom so that you can be one of the 4 percent that will still be open after ten years, so that you will be able to walk away with what your intention was in the first place, and so that the fruits of your labor finally gave you the financial freedom that you so much wanted to achieve, which in turn allowed you to have your personal freedom.

WHAT DID I LEARN?

1) You have to know how to separate the relationship between your life and your business from the get go.

    The business has to be a part of your life but not your whole life. Otherwise, it will consume you. You have to create a business that allows you the time to give you the life style you want. The business should be a vehicle for you to achieve the life style, the sense of fulfillment, and the satisfaction that you want. (After all is not that one of the reasons you went into business for yourself?) So stop treating your business as your life style and start treating it as the part of your whole life style that is going to be used as the vehicle to achieve the kind of life you want to lead. You do have other jobs — you may be a dad, mom, husband — and you may have interests like reading, golfing, and volunteering. Balance is important, reflection is important, being able to look at situations from outside is important, clearing your mind is important — all these other activities allow you to be more effective at anything you do.

2) You must work on your business, not in it.

The question that you need to ask yourself is, "Are there any areas in my business that I am working in that are unnecessary and are there areas in my business that I could be working on that will and could bring me better returns?" If the answer is yes, then you are probably doing work that you can pay somebody else to do, in which case you are not focusing on the important areas of your business. You have to think that you are creating a business that can run without you.

3) You must systemize your business with the right plans, policies, and procedures in place.

What I am trying to say is that you must approach your business as though it were a franchise. The mortality rate for franchises is exactly the opposite. In other words, 80 percent work. If you go into a Taco Bell in Mobile, Alabama, and then another one in Seattle, Washington, they will both be run the same way, their food will be the same, their look will be the same; everything is all spelled out. In other words, every item from look to food to service has been documented and systemized. Thus, the system runs the operation, not the employees. Did you know that the employee turnover rate in the fast food business is 200 percent per year? Yet, a store like McDonald's runs like a well-oiled machine. Why do you think that is? Most owners organize their business around the people they have, and when there are problems, they blame their people for the poor results. Thus, if a business is successful, then it takes extraordinary people in this case to make them work. However, in the most successful businesses, most owners do not realize that systems run the business and ordinary people run the systems.

4) You must be able to strategize and implement.

In other words, once you have decided what your business is all about, then you have to determine through strategy what your goal is in the business. Based on the different aspects of your business, you have to come up with strategies that will allow you to achieve the desired results in a systematic way. Once this is determined, you have to implement these strategies through actions that you have outlined in order to achieve and track your desired results. Most business owners are reactive, not proactive. With a predetermined strategy you automatically become proactive, which always keeps you ahead of the game, rather than trying to react to issues that come up without you having anticipated your course of action. You must understand that you cannot have a strategy and then not implement — no results. You cannot solve issues as they occur without a plan; otherwise you will be forever putting out fires and working in your business rather than on your business. Both the above approaches go hand in hand. Thus, the smart business owner will develop the system with plans, policies, and procedures and then give his or her people the right training and tools to implement these procedures based on the strategy outlined and then empower them to take the initiative to use their training to achieve the desired results. You have to think of this as a long distance running race where you as the runner need to know how to pace yourself so that you can pick up the speed at the right time to achieve that goal of winning.

5) Be detail oriented and work on all aspects of the business in small increments so that the whole puzzle comes together more easily.

Whether you are a small business or a large business, in order to be successful all businesses have to keep a watchful eye on several different aspects of the business. Being in the hospitality and food service business, the best analogy is the build up of an entrée. Before you take it to the table to create the wow factor for the guest, you have put some planning into developing that entrée. Take into consideration the ingredients, the spice levels, the accompaniments that will complement the dish, if the price point makes it seem like the guest is getting their money's worth, how it is presented, how busy the kitchen is and decide if you will be able to put the dish together in a timely fashion. Then, once you have answered all these questions, you have to start with the right ingredients, make sure they are fresh, make sure you follow the right method of cooking it, make sure the same is happening to the accompaniments, and make sure there is synergy between you as the chef and your sous chef. Then you have to present it on the plate, make sure the wait person takes it to the table in a timely manner and places it in just the right way on the table so that the guest will look at it and say, "Wow." Then hopefully he or she takes a bite and says, "Wow" again. The service has to be impeccable and the whole dining experience has to be a good one. Without all the above falling into place like a well-oiled machine, you will not achieve the desired results.

If your business is going to be successful, there are several key factors that need to have constant attention. These key factors have to be constantly evaluated for effectiveness and worked on in detail in order to be effective. These are:

a) Your leadership skills

b) The company management makeup

c) How you control the financial side of the business

d) Your business operations

e) How you market your product or service

Without being consistent about evaluating, improving, and quantifying each of these areas you will have trouble running a well-oiled machine. As the owner, you should spend time once a week on each of the categories reflecting, evaluating, quantifying, and then, based on this, executing so that you are always in touch with the pulse of the business. Depending on the size, you may have people in charge of each of these sectors or you may be wearing several hats yourself. In either case a minimum of a one hour reflection on each of these factors at least once a week is a must.

So how do you keep ahead of the curve and have a business that is not only successful but be able to continually sustain its success and improve all the time? The first thing to recognize is that you do not know everything. A lot of business owners have a high ego and do not understand the meaning of "the best man for the best job." You may not have the luxury of hiring that person; however, if you set aside that ego and are open to learning and improving there is a lot you can do to still be able to achieve the success that you deserve. Because you work hard, you should be able to reap the rewards of that time and effort. So what are some of the things you can do to help you in your journey to success?

a) Find a mentor, somebody you know that would fit the role, and if not, somebody that you can hire to keep you in check. A good mentor will be able to save you a tremendous amount of heartache, guide you through your failures and successes, and be able to tell you what not to do. This saves you a lot of time and effort, as the mentor will look at you with a fresh pair of eyes. Because he or she is not involved in the ownership of your business, he or she can look at you objectively and give you sound advice.

b) Make sure you build a competent team. You need to stick to what you do best and hire the right combination of people to allow you to get the job done in the most effective way.

c) Surround yourself with like-minded people, whether they are in your industry or not and get together with them once a month to discuss issues. Learn from what they are doing. Even if you get one pointer to improve what you are doing every time you talk, can you imagine the advantage you have over other people who do not have this opportunity? It is invaluable. With this you not only will get ideas but you might even get a contact that will allow you to propel to the next level.

d) Make sure you have the right tools and the best tools to use so that you are at the leading edge of the system you have created. This is called best practices.

This brings us to a very important item that we talked about earlier: systems. I have been doing this for the last 25 years, and I can tell you that there are very few original ideas. I can also tell you that somewhere out there somebody is doing what you want to do and doing it quite well. Put aside that ego and study. Implement and execute.

Putu Knutte

Company	Bali Wine Bar & Grill
Address	2416 18th Street Sacramento, CA 95818
Role in Company	Owner / Partner
E-mail	baligrill@sbcglobal
Web site	**www.baligrill.net**
Phone	916-444-1247

Background

Putu Knutte has been in restaurant management for over ten years. Besides her current restaurant, she also worked for a four to five star restaurant. Her first job in the hospitality field was as a busser.

Career

Putu Knutte is owner of Bali Wine Bar & Grill in Sacramento, California. She is an active member of the Sacramento Chamber of Commerce. She manages six employees and says her ideal employee possesses a good work ethic, quality skills, and is a fast learner. She believes giving good training and direction is what makes a good manager. She does not have a specific management style, but is able to work with her employees and believes that is something that sets her apart.

The toughest lesson Putu has had to learn in her management career is learning to run everything. The piece of advice she wishes she was given when she first started in management was to have passion and work hard. She was lucky to receive free lessons and advice from her husband (who is also her partner in the restaurant). He has been in the hospitality business for over 30 years.

In the next five or ten years Putu's goal is to open two more restaurants.

A Little Restaurant Information

Bali Wine Bar & Grill serves authentic Balinese cuisine. The restaurant's hours are A) Lunch: Monday through Saturday from 11:30 a.m. to 2:30 p.m. and B) Dinner: Sunday through Thursday from 5:30 p.m. to 9 p.m. and Friday and Saturday from 5:30 p.m. to 10 p.m. Their busiest hours are the dinner times on Fridays and Saturdays.

They accept reservations but do not have valet parking. The restaurant does serve alcohol, which Putu says plays an important role in the business. She also believes colors affect the appetite. Customer checks do not include gratuity.

Putu says their older crowd, with an average age of 35 and older, is what sets her restaurant apart and draws in clients. Once a month they also put on an event called Culture Night. They also offer catering.

When it comes to the food, 100 percent of the food arrives fresh. They do buy their fresh foods from local vendors. A computer is used to keep the daily records of the restaurant. Dishes are done by machine, and they hire a company to check their dishwasher and supplies monthly. They hire an outside company for laundry.

For the staff, Putu does require they adhere to a dress code. The dress code is a long sleeve shirt of any color with black pants. Men are not required to wear ties. They do not have a host or hostess. She does use flex scheduling.

Putu does step in and help when an employee is missing. She says she helps with everything: helping prep, doing dishes, waiting tables, bussing, serving, and basically anything she needs to do to run the restaurant.

She has never had to adjust prices because of competition. The markup for the restaurant is 21/2, and to keep costs down she minimizes the labor. To minimize accidents in the restaurant, she says they keep everything clean and put staff in the right places, as well as keep an eye on everything.

When a customer is unhappy with the service at the restaurant, they will give the customer a gift certificate to get them to come back and try again. When the customers are unhappy with the food, they will be given another dish or a complimentary dessert. She does reward frequent diners, and coupons are placed in some of their advertising.

Putu says the restaurant has fulfilled her dream of what it should be, and if she had to do it all over again, she said yes, as she is already working toward another restaurant.

Advice Tidbit

"Keep your labor costs down."

Kristopher A. Kotte

Company	Bon Appetit at the Art Institute of Chicago
Address	111 South Michigan Avenue Chicago, IL 60603
Role in Company	General Manager
E-mail	Kris.Kotte@cafebonappetit.com
Web site	**artic.edu, bamco.com**
Phone	321-443-7274
Fax	312-263-0697

BON APPÉTIT
MANAGEMENT COMPANY
food services for a sustainable future

Background

Kristopher Kotte has been in the restaurant industry for 20 years and in management for 19 years. Besides his current employment at Bon Appetit he also worked for places such as Giordano's, Northside Café, Redfish, Famous Dave's, Riva Restaurant on Navy Pier, Café Concepts and Management, and Entourage on American Lane. His first job was at Giordano's. Becoming a restaurant manager was not a conscious decision for him until after a few years and considerable success in the field.

"I liked the multifaceted nature of the industry and the absolute control of your own destiny from an enterprise standpoint."

Career

Kristopher does not own his own restaurant, but manages upwards of 200 employees at Bon Appetit at the Art Institute of Chicago. The restaurant's estimated sales from 2006 were approximately $10 million.

His ideal employee possesses an even temperament, intelligence, an inquisitive nature, passion, and theory. He believes it takes patience, open-mindedness, and tenacity to be a good manager. The qualities he believes he possesses that help in his management career are the qualities listed above, as well as a strong interest in organizational management, which gives him a more business-minded approach rather than a typical restaurant approach.

Kristopher's specific management style includes educating, empowering, and providing accountability. He tries to teach individuality and life skills that go beyond the restaurant group.

"In this fluid of an industry, you are lucky to have great employees for more than a year so I feel it is my job to positively impact everyone I touch and make them marketable and valuable for myself and for the next phase they enter."

The best piece of advice Kristopher was given when he first started in his management career was to be a leader in every facet possible and do his homework and get people on his side. The toughest lesson he has had to learn so far is that bad things happen to good people.

"Everyone takes their bullets at some time and even a successful place can shut down tomorrow."

The advice Kristopher wishes he had been given when he started was to leave nothing to interpretation in the end.

"Solicitation of opinion is critical in the conceptualization phase, but after implementation there should be only one unified vision and, to the greatest degree possible, complete thematic congruency."

Something he has accomplished so far in his career has been to guide dramatic change in profitability, sales, and employee relations in every position he has held. In the next five to ten years he would like to be the RVP or CEO of a $100 to $150 million territory or company. He has managed to be part of change at Bon Appetit, but believes the restaurant does not have any major changes in its future.

"Every work situation I have come into has included a major paradigm shift in its thinking. I have consistently demanded that the rank and file and the management have an idea of the vision and mission of the company. That goes beyond just reading the mission statement and hanging it by the time clock, but by investing an individual's workload into their little part of the mission statement and direction. I believe it is critical to teach the 'whys' behind the 'hows.'

"I believe a good plan requires very few changes. Change really should have to happen only if drastic changes happen in market conditions (i.e., 9/11). Our primary concern is to just manage change and adapt so good planning builds in some air that a plan can evolve but not require major change. Therefore, I am pretty comfortable with our plan and believe that there is not any 'change' on the radar."

A Little Restaurant Information

Bon Appetit serves a variety of foods, but focuses mainly on comfort classics done with a French technique that highlight global flavor influences. The restaurant is actually divided into two areas: The Garden Restaurant and The Artist's Café. The Garden Restaurant's hours are Monday through Sunday from 11:30 a.m. to 3 p.m. and summer hours on Thursday and Friday music nights from 11:30 a.m. to 9 p.m. The Artist's Café's hours are Monday through Sunday from 11 a.m. to 4 p.m., except Thursday when they are open until 7 p.m. and summer hours, which are subject to change on Thursday and Friday nights. Their busiest time is from noon to 2 p.m. They do accept reservations but do not have valet parking. Bouncers are not required since the museum has plenty of security stationed in their area.

They serve alcohol, and Kristopher says it is important to the business, although not as important as he has seen it be in other places he has worked. Their being in a world-class museum and cultural center makes the restaurant unique and helps it stand apart as it adds value. They also offer catering.

They are members of many of their local civic groups, including CCTB (Chicago Convention and Tourism Bureau), MPI (Meeting Planners International), NACE (National Association of Catering Executives), and IFSEA (International Food Service Executives Association).

One hundred percent of their food arrives fresh, as they follow the Monterey Bay Seafood Watch requirements religiously. They purchase their fresh foods locally.

"We have corporate-wide programs to support sustainability and local farming. Two program examples are Farm to Fork and Eat Local."

The age group that prefers the restaurant is the 35 to 50 year old range. They have absolutely had to adjust pricing because of the competition before, and Kris says training and education is the best way to keep their costs down. Their markup is typically three times overall, but that varies by department and revenue center.

When customers are unsatisfied they attempt to correct every problem the minute it is identified. They are not shy about making people happy but do not bend over backwards — to the extent which they are able to accommodate their customer they do. When there are six or more customers at the table, the check will include gratuity as well as for à la carte operations and all events. They do not formally reward their frequent diners, but they are currently addressing the possibility. They do not offer coupons in their advertising.

When it comes to his staff, Kristopher has occasionally had to step in for them. There is a host and hostess on every shift, and these staff members do have some managerial duties over other staff members, but in a very limited scope. The staff is required to follow a dress code, which includes dress slacks, ties, and dress shirts. He does use flex scheduling for his employees. The kitchen staff is evaluated by making them accountable to their job descriptions.

"Also, by the amount of personal growth shown, such as learning a new position, and achieving personal goals, such as running a marathon, losing weight, stopping smoking, and going back to school, among others."

They evaluate the wait staff much the same way as the kitchen staff, but are also held a little more accountable in hard terms, such as check averages, sales, and so on. To handle staff squabbles, Kristopher goes about it mainly on the front end by being thorough and attentive to their lives and needs.

"We are fortunate to not have much turmoil. The staff does a lot of self-policing and protecting the greater good. A bad seed won't get far with their peers."

Outside companies provide many professional services, including food and beverage vendors, commercial cleaning, some human resources, and placement outsourcing. They use a computer to keep the daily records of the restaurant. Although they do some make-do when it comes to their equipment, Kristopher says there is always some in the industry, but they are fortunate to be very well-supplied. An industrial machine is used to wash the dishes, and they have taken many steps to help prevent accidents in their establishments.

"Steps include extensive on-going training and awareness, tracking accidents on a very visible board, cutting gloves, and 100 percent use of approved, non-slip shoes."

If Kristopher had it to do all over again he said yes he would. Although he is new to his current operation, he says they are close to reaching their goal of what they want the restaurant to be. They still have some work to do.

"By the end of the year I expect to be as efficient as the physical plant will allow."

Advice Tidbits

"Understand your place, ask a lot of questions, be open-minded yet mentally critical of yourself and what you are doing and good things will come. Young people in this industry fail because they fall short of one or more of those attributes and expect things for which they are unprepared."

Michael Larey

Company	One-Eyed Jack's Restaurant & Saloon
Address	1201 Dixie Overland Rd. Bossier City, LA 71111
Role in Company	Director of Operations
E-mail	michaellarey@one-eyedjacks.net
Web site	**www.one-eyedjacks.net**
Phone	318-549-4990
Fax	318-549-4992

About Michael Larey

The kitchen was always the gathering place during his childhood. It did not matter if it was at the family plantation in Louisiana or the farmhouse in Arkansas. Although not formally trained, Michael Larey has devoted much time to working with and observing techniques of great chefs in restaurants all over the south from New Orleans to Memphis. The inspiration to open One-Eyed Jacks Restaurant and Saloon came when Michael was serving with the Louisiana Army National Guard in Iraq. The menu at One-Eyed Jack's is All-American featuring mouth watering steaks, slow smoked ribs, or even flame grilled shrimp and tuna. Everything at the restaurant is made from scratch; even the bread is freshly baked. The food is unforgettable; the building is remarkable, and with some of the most scenic views available in the Ark-La-Tex, it is a must see destination.

Background

Michael Larey has been in the restaurant industry for ten years and in management for five years. Besides One-Eyed Jack's Restaurant & Saloon, Michael has also worked at places like Cuco's, Chit's Hoppin Hacienda, Posados Cafe, Java Blues, Insomniacs, and Market Street Deli. His first job in the hospitality field was as a waiter. He decided to become a restaurant manager because he liked the fast pace and never-ending challenges.

Career

Michael is Director of Operations for the restaurant he owns, One-Eyed Jack's Restaurant & Saloon. He manages 50 employees and finds the ability to speak for themselves, being flexible, and giving their best are the qualities that his ideal employee possesses.

Michael believes quick decision-making and the ability to simplify complicated situations is what it takes to be a good manager. He says his enjoying people, handling large amounts of stress, and being good with young people are the qualities he possesses that make him a good manager. His specific management style is inclusive, as he says he always makes sure to include and acknowledge any input he gets from his people.

The toughest lesson Michael has learned while in his management career has been that even the people you trust the most will take from you if you make it too easy. He wishes when he had started in management that someone had stressed organization to him. The best piece of advice he was given when he first started happened on a bad night when he was upset with himself and his crew over their performance.

"My GM pulled me aside and explained to me that not every mistake is to be taken as a personal defeat; rather it should be looked at as an opportunity to improve."

Michael has set some goals for the restaurant. In five years he wants to have created a system that does his work for him. In ten years he wants to be retired.

A Little Restaurant Information

One-Eyed Jack's Restaurant & Saloon serves American food like steaks, shrimp, and barbeque. They are open from 11 a.m. to 9 p.m. on Sunday through Wednesday and from 11 a.m. to midnight on Thursday through Saturday. Their busiest hour is 7 p.m. They do serve alcohol, and Michael says it is an important aspect to the business. Reservations are accepted, but they do not have valet parking or have a need for bouncers.

Their customer crowd is a diverse group that Michael says causes everyone to feel very welcome. They also have live music on Fridays and Saturdays, karaoke on Thursdays, and video poker available. They do catering as well. They belong to the Bossier City Chamber of Commerce, Louisiana Restaurant Association, and the Veterans of Foreign Wars.

A computer is used to keep the daily records of the restaurant. Dishes are washed by a machine. Michael says they always make sure to have proper equipment and never try to just make-do. They only hire outside companies for their accounting and laundry.

All the food at One-Eyed Jack's Restaurant & Saloon is prepared fresh from scratch using traditional southern recipes. The only food item that is purchased frozen is their shrimp. They do buy their fresh foods locally. They have had to adjust their pricing because of competition before but find the best way to cut costs in the restaurant is by watching the inventory and staff.

To satisfy a customer who is unhappy with the food, service, or atmosphere, Michael says they will do whatever they can within reason to make them happy. Gratuity is only included on checks for large groups. Frequent diners at One-Eyed Jack's are rewarded through e-mail coupons, birthday and anniversary rewards, and sometimes Michael will go into the kitchen and make a special dessert or appetizer.

The most important trait Michael looks for in his wait staff is their ability to talk to people with ease. They do have a host/hostess, but this member of the staff does not have any managerial duties over the other employees.

They do flex scheduling for the employees, and they are required to follow a dress code, which includes One-Eyed Jacks branded merchandise. The men are not required to wear ties. Michael evaluates his kitchen staff by their performance and his wait staff by their performance and input from customers. He says he has had to step in for members of his staff before.

When asked if he thought One-Eyed Jack's Restaurant & Saloon had fulfilled his dream of what it should be, Michael said not yet.

Advice Tidbits

"Always have faith in yourself and your people. Manage your people individually. Not everyone responds to the same input."

Mary Madison

Company	Lagniappe
	(A Creole Cajun Joynt)
Address	1525 West 79th Street
	Chicago, IL 60620
Role in Company	Managing Member / Chef
E-mail	Lagniappe26@aol.com
Web site	**cajunjoynt.com**
Phone	773-994-6375
Fax	773-285-9001

Background

Mary Dionne Madison has been in the restaurant industry for three years. She has been in management for 15 years, with the last three being in the hospitality field. Besides her current employment at Lagniappe, Mary has also worked for The Bay, which is located in Chicago. She always wanted to be a restaurant manager and stumbled into being chef/owner after the initial chef was not in line with the vision of the establishment prior to opening.

Mary was born in 1968 in Chicago, Illinois. She is a Chemistry graduate of Xavier University in New Orleans, Louisiana. Her love of cooking started at the young age of five when early one Saturday morning she was discovered by her mother standing on a chair in front of the stove with cast iron skillets, blazing flames, half-cooked bacon, and scorched eggs. She told her mother, "I'm cooking breakfast, Mama." From there, her parents decided to limit her cooking endeavors to a ball of dough and an Easy Bake Oven. She was able to cook a full course meal by the age of eleven.

Career

Mary owns her own restaurant, Lagniappe — A Creole Cajun Joynt, where she manages six employees. Her ideal employee possesses willingness, flexibility, charisma, and problem solving skills. She believes it takes

---

adaptability, versatility, an ability to be hands on, and training to be a good manager. She believes she has most of those qualities, which help her in her management career. She does not have one specific management style; rather she says she bases it on each individual she manages. Her one-on-one coaching of her employees is one of her unique management techniques.

The toughest lesson Mary has learned in her management career is how most of her employees have an inability to separate their personal and social issues from the workplace. The best piece of advice she was given when she first started in management was to be confident, determined, and courageous. She wishes someone had told her what a hard business it is.

Mary's goals for the next five or ten years are to synergize entertainment and to expand the restaurant within the corporate marketplace. She has been acknowledged for her participation in community service (helping to feed the poor of Chicago) and was awarded the Chicago Tribune's Good Eats Award 2006. Within the first year of opening the restaurant, they were voted 29th out of 100 Best Things Eaten by Time Out Chicago in 2005. They were also featured on Channel 7's Hungry Hound 2006, Taste of Chicago 2006, and were featured on every major media market.

Mary had to implement a change when the management and employees were not meeting expectations. The immediate manager she had brought in was not meeting the goals of the restaurant, and the employees had become disgruntled. She fired everyone and started over. Now she has the right mix of people working for her and says they blend together for a harmonious atmosphere. A change she wants to implement next is expanding to breakfast and having live entertainment.

A Little Restaurant Information

Lagniappe — A Creole Cajun Joynt serves Louisiana-style Creole and Cajun food. They are open Tuesday, Wednesday, and Thursday from 11 a.m. to 8 p.m. and Friday and Saturday from 11 a.m. to 10 p.m. Their busiest hours are midday and evening, and they do accept reservations. They also do catering.

Lagniappe does not require bouncers, but they do offer valet parking when they are having functions. They currently do not serve alcohol but are planning to in the near future, and Mary says it will be important to the business. Its authentic food and upscale atmosphere are what sets the restaurant apart and draws in its clientele. They have televisions and also offer a private party room.

All the food at Lagniappe is made fresh. The only food item that arrives frozen is the seafood. They buy their fresh foods locally. They have never had to adjust their pricing because of competition. Their markup is anywhere from 1.5 to 2.5. Mary has found the best way to keep their costs down is by cooking only from scratch.

The customer base for Lagniappe ranges from young adult to middle age. When one of the customers is unsatisfied with the service, Mary tries to sympathize with the situation. When a customer is unhappy with the food, she will compensate for it, and when a customer is unhappy with the atmosphere, Mary will extend additional courtesies to try and satisfy the customer. Customer checks to do not include gratuity. They do reward frequent diners — rewards are based on a reward card system they have and the accumulation of points for items — and offer coupons in advertising.

When it comes to her staff, Mary looks for wait staff members that have good people skills and proper etiquette. She has had to step in for members of her staff before. They do have a host/ hostess but that member of the staff does not have managerial duties over the other staff members. She does not use flex scheduling for her employees, but does require a dress code, which includes shirts and black pants. However, men are not required to wear ties. Mary evaluates the staff by featuring them in media bites and giving them encouragement. So far there have been no staff squabbles, but if there are, Mary says she will handle it with mediation.

Lagniappe uses a computer to keep up with the daily records of the restaurant. They only hire an outside company for their knife sharpening. Mary says they have all the equipment they need for the restaurant and do not have to do any make-do. They wash all dishes by hand. To reduce accidents in the restaurant, they mitigate any possible hazards.

When asked if Lagniappe had reached her goal of what she thought it would be, Mary said it has actually exceeded it. She would never have thought that so many levels of achievement and acknowledgements would have occurred. If she had to go back and do it all over again, she says she would.

"It was God's will."

Advice Tidbits

"Keep up with your training and with the business plan and goals."

Humberto Martinez Jr.

Company	Timothy O'Toole's Pub
Address	622 N. Fairbanks Ct. Chicago, IL 60611
Role in Company	President
E-mail	Pub622@sbcglobal.net
Web site	**Timothyotooles.com**
Phone	312-642-0700
Fax	312-642-6848

Background

Humberto Martinez Jr. has been in the restaurant industry for 25 years and in management for 20 of those years. He now owns his own restaurant, Timothy O'Toole's Pub. Besides his current restaurant, Humberto has also worked for companies such as Monroe Club, Pastability, New Image, Bistro 1800, Lava Lounge, and more. His first job in the restaurant industry was as a busboy. He says that becoming a restaurant manager was "a natural progression in the business" that he loves.

Career

Humberto manages 100 employees at Timothy O'Toole's Pub. His ideal employee will possess qualities such as punctuality, dependability, a good sense of humor, and self respect.

He believes patience, good decision-making skills, and the ability to stay calm in any situation are what it takes to be a good manager. Humberto believes being a good people person is one of his qualities that help him with his management career. His management style is very hands on. He also has an open-door policy 24 hours a day, seven days a week.

One of the toughest lessons he has learned in his career has been that not all people are honest and they do not always have your best interest at heart. The one piece of advice Humberto wishes he had been given when he first started in management was to be prepared for the amount of hours required. The best piece of advice he was given when he started was "patience, patience, patience." When asked about his goals for the next five or ten years, he said this:

"They are always the same: Continue to grow the business while enjoying what I am doing and be the best person while doing it."

Humberto has won several awards for different aspects of his business. He is very proud of being recognized as Best Sports Bar in Chicago, for receiving awards for some of his recipes by the American Heart Association, receiving awards in Chicago Wingfest, and being named Top Sports Bar by numerous publications. His 2006 sales were estimated at $3.5 million.

A Little Restaurant Information

Timothy O'Toole's Pub serves American/pub food, and they do offer catering as well. The restaurant is open from 11 a.m. to 3 a.m. Their busiest hours are from 6 p.m. to 8 p.m. Reservations are taken on a limited basis, and they do offer valet parking. They do serve alcohol, and Humberto says it is important to the business. To draw in clients, he says being top quality with a great atmosphere that caters to all ages sets Timothy O'Toole's apart.

"We also offer plenty of activities to keep the customer busy and interactive."

The restaurant has pool tables, video games, darts, Golden Tee, 45 televisions, Karaoke Nights, and NTN Interactive Trivia, as well as many contests and giveaways. They are a member of their local Chambers of Commerce: GNMAC, Streeterville Chamber of Commerce, and Illinois Restaurant Association.

When it comes to the food served at Timothy O'Toole's Pub, 20 percent of the food arrives fresh and 80 percent frozen. They do buy their fresh food from local vendors. Humberto says they have never had to adjust prices due to competition. Their markup is about three times. Outside companies are hired to do some of the restaurant duties, such as laundry, accounting, and so on. A computer is used to keep the restaurant's daily records. Dishes are done by machine. Humberto has found the best ways to keep costs down are loss prevention and good implementation of portion control with both food and liquor.

The most important trait Humberto looks for in his wait staff is friendliness and an overall good personality. He occasionally does have to step in for his employees as a cook or waiter. The restaurant does have a host/hostess who does have managerial duties in a limited capacity over other members of the staff. Security personnel are also employed and are used in a hosting capacity. A dress code is in effect for the staff, but the men are not required to wear ties. They do not use flex scheduling. The kitchen and wait staff are evaluated during planned yearly evaluations.

To handle staff squabbles, Humberto will sit the individuals down with their direct supervisor. Then they will listen, evaluate, and find a reasonable solution.

Sometimes the checks include gratuity. They do offer rewards to frequent diners and coupons in advertising. Humberto tries to satisfy his customers who may be unhappy.

"It depends on the situation, but we always strive to ensure a positive experience for our customers. With the food, we replace the item or offer a different item. Whatever it takes to make the customer happy. With the atmosphere, we offer so many different options that we rarely have this occur."

To reduce accidents in his establishment they participate in safety meetings, have an extensive use of mats, ensure use of proper footwear, and use cautions signs on wet floors.

Humberto says his restaurant has fulfilled his dream of what it should be, but says there is still more to come. When asked if he had to do it all over again would he, he said "in a heartbeat."

Advice Tidbits

"Each day is unique, and our hours are very long and unpredictable. It's important to have passion for the business."

Jaime Miller

Company	Remember That Chef, In Home Dining & Personal Chef Services
Address	40 Grandville Ave. Suite, 1510 Hamilton, Ontario L8E 1J7
Role in Company	Chef / Owner
E-mail	Jaime@rememberthatchef.ca
Web site	**www.rememberthatchef.ca**
Phone	905-560-6924
Fax	905-650-9795

Remember That Chef
In home dining &
Personal chef services

Background

Jaime Miller is the chef and owner of Remember That Chef in Canada. It is an in-home dining and personal chef service (catering). He has been in the restaurant industry for over 20 years and in management for six years so far. Besides his current restaurant, he has also worked at Bo Chins, Royal York Hotel, Holiday Inn, Liuna Gardens Banquet Center, Kelsey's Road House, Good Sheppard, Stinson House Bistro, La Boheme Bistro, and Emma's Back Porch Bar and Grill. His first job in the hospitality field was at Bo Chins Chinese as a prep cook where he says he learned how not to cut his fingers with a cleaver. He decided to become a manager because of the ability to take charge and to be able to do food the way he felt it should be done.

"Many places I've watched them just plate food with no consistency or it looks unappealing when it goes out. People pay good money for their food. I'd take the extra five minutes and plate it right. Also I want them to remember us and come again."

Career

Jaime manages 10 to 15 employees at Remember That Chef. The qualities his ideal employee possesses are honesty, being on time and dressed in uniform when arriving to work, being approachable, and having a willingness to learn.

He believes a sense of humor, willingness to teach, patience, understanding, and respect are what it takes to be a good manager. He says the qualities he has that help him in his management career are understanding, listening, teaching, respect, and the ability to admit he is wrong. His management style is being straightforward. Something he does that is unique in his management is having fun and working as a team.

The toughest lesson Jaime has had to learn while in management is taking orders from people who really did not know what they were talking about. When he first started in management the advice he wishes he was given was to not talk back even if he was right.

"When I was the chef at the Good Sheppard after a year and a half it felt like the more I did the more they wanted. When told that one person didn't like liver, I was told to take it off the menu. The other 30 tenants still ate the liver. Three months later my boss asked me why there was no liver. I told her that she had requested not to serve it again. Her response was, 'NO, I never said that, but start serving it again.' So I put it back on the menu and had to serve another meat for the ones that didn't like liver. After three years there they let me go. Why? Because I wasn't putting up with their politics and they said I had a bad attitude toward some tenants."

The best piece of advice he was given when he first started was to treat the tenants like they were normal people. The place he worked in, The Good Sheppard, was for people who had disabilities. These people were almost to the point where they could go live out on their own, but still needed consulting, which they provided 24 hours a day.

While Jaime was at The Good Sheppard, he was acknowledged for his clean kitchen, always passing inspection, and for the food. So far at Remember That Chef, the clients are raving about the food. He has testimonials from his clients acknowledging the food (you can see some of these on his Web site). Something he has accomplished so far in his career that is he proud of has been opening his own business while other people laughed at him and told him he was wasting his money and time. He did it anyway.

"Slowly I'm building my business and learning from my mistakes."

Jaime's goal for the coming years is to expand his Remember That Chef business so that it becomes a household name.

A Little Restaurant Information

Chef Jaime with sister Andrea

Remember That Chef's hours are based on when their client's events take place. They are usually busiest during 3 and 7 p.m. The menus are tailored to their customer's likes and dislikes. They go to their clients home and prepare their meal. Alcohol is served if the client provides it, and any activity, such as musicians or clowns, are provided if the client would like. Most of their clients are 30 years old and over. Remember That Chef is a member of the Burlington Chamber of Commerce and of the Canadian Personal Chef Alliance.

Jaime describes the cuisine they serve as bistro to fine dining. All the foods used to prepare the dishes are bought fresh the day of the event. They use local suppliers.

"Our fruit and vegetables are purchased from organic and local farms in the area. (Farm Fresh) Meats are from Nardni's Specialty, and the seafood is from Dave's Fish Market."

To keep costs down, Jaime shops at the Bulk Barn and purchases food from local suppliers. He has reduced his prices to compete with competition before.

"I'm very flexible with prices. I try and work with the customer."

Although he has not had any customers unhappy with their service or food, Jaime says if they did, he would offer them a dinner for free. He rewards a client after five bookings with him by giving them a free dinner for two. They do not yet offer coupons in advertising.

The most important traits Jaime looks for in his wait staff is being able to work independently, friendliness, and dependability. His servers and bartenders are required to wear white dress shirts, black dress pants, and a bow tie or black tie. The chefs are required to wear a chef jacket and black or design-patterned pants. Jaime has had to step in for an employee before.

"One time I was doing a wedding for 25 people in their home. I arrived at 1 p.m. to start the preparation of the food. My server was to be there at 3 p.m. to start with the hors d'oeuvres. At 3:30 I called her thinking she might have gotten lost or was running behind. Her boyfriend said he would pass the message on and have her call me. No reply! She never showed up so I also become the host. Thankfully, some of the guests that attended their wedding helped out in the kitchen and helped clean up. I received an unbelievable testimonial from

them. To view their testimonials visit my Web site **www.rememberthatchef. ca** *under testimonial from Diane."*

Jaime evaluates his kitchen staff by their knowledge of the food, how well they work and clean (an example is whether they wipe food from the table onto the floor instead of into the trash), and by any comments he receives from clients on their performance. For his wait staff he evaluates their cleaning and from the comments received from clients on their performance. To handle staff squabbles, he will ask the parties involved to go get a cup of coffee and then meet him in his office so they can sit down and talk.

"There are always three sides to a story. I'll listen to both sides of their story and then give my opinion. Most of the time we all end up laughing at the problem."

To wash the dishes most times he uses the dishwasher of the client, unless they do not have one. Then they do the dishes by hand. As for his equipment, he says most of the time the clients have the pots and pans on hand to use. Occasionally he has had to bring along a cuisiart.

"I always bring my bag of herbs and spices, knives, vinegars and oils, meat tenderizer, and other kitchen gadgets. My bag weighs about 25 to 30 pounds. You never know what to expect going into someone's home."

When asked if his business had fulfilled everything he felt it should be, Jaime said, since he is everything from the bookkeeper to the chef, he does not believe so because there is still a lot of learning for him to do. Finally, when Jaime was asked if he had to do it all over again would he, he replied yes.

"Owning your own business is the way to go. Mind you I would have learned not to make so many mistakes in the beginning."

Advice Tidbits

"Do not yell at someone in public. If there's a problem, take them back into the office. Many times I have seen others being yelled at in the restaurant or in the kitchen in front of the public or staff. Never do it in the restaurant! What are your customers going to think? In the kitchen why embarrass them? If the manager has something to say do it behind doors. No one likes being yelled at especially in view of customers or staff."

Stephanie Morley

Company	Ninety-Nine Restaurant
Address	20 MacArthur Blvd. Coventry, RI 02816
Role in Company	Assistant Manager
E-mail	smorin11@cox.net
Phone	401-615-1673

Background

Stephanie Morley has been in the restaurant industry for 12 years. She has been in management for nine of those years. Currently, she is assistant manager for Ninety-Nine Restaurant. She has been the assistant manager there for two years. Besides the Ninety-Nine, she has also worked at Appetite's Family Restaurant and TGI Friday's. Her first job in the hospitality field was at Appetite's Family Restaurant as a cashier and waitress. The reason she got into management is that she loved the pace of the restaurant and dealing with customers and knew there was a great potential for advancement.

Career

Stephanie does not own her own restaurant, but as assistant manager at the Ninety-Nine, she manages around 65 employees. Her ideal employee is hardworking and energetic and cares about the guests. She believes patience, understanding, consistency, and accountability are what it takes to be a good manager. Stephanie says she is a very hard worker who cares about her guests and employees. She enjoys working around food and loves teaching others new things. She says all these things are what make her a good manager.

"I am tough and expect a lot from my employees, but as long as they are doing the right thing, I like to have fun, too."

Something unique Stephanie does when it comes to managing her employees is playing games and having contests on a daily basis. The toughest lesson she has learned while in management has been that everyone is different.

"You have to handle each person in a different way while still being consistent across the board."

Something Stephanie has done in her management career so far that she is proud of is the long way she has come in dealing with employee relations and how she has learned through doing. She recently implemented some new policies involving the handling of guest complaints. She also has helped in many changes with the organization of the management staff.

In the next five to ten years Stephanie would like to become a general manager of a Ninety-Nine Restaurant (there are currently 122 locations). She would eventually like to be a training general manager and run a successful store.

A Little Restaurant Information

Ninety-Nine Restaurant serves American food — mainly steaks and seafood — and they are famous for their boneless buffalo wings. Their estimated 2006 sales are about $1,600,000. There are currently 122 locations of the Ninety-Nine Restaurant throughout New England, New York, Pennsylvania, and New Jersey. Stephanie's store is open on Monday, Tuesday, and Wednesday from 11:30 a.m. to 11 p.m. On Thursday, Friday, and Saturday they are open from 11:30 a.m. to midnight. On Sundays, they are open from 11:30 a.m. to 10 pm. Their busiest hour is from 5:30 to 6:30.

They do serve alcohol, and it is important to their business, as it is currently 19 percent of sales. Their goal is to bring it up to 22 percent of sales. Stephanie says that their family atmosphere and the huge variety of their great food is what sets their restaurant apart and draws clients in. Although they do not cater, they do offer platters for takeout. They do not take reservations, but do accept call-ahead seating. The age group that seems to prefer the restaurant is 30 to 45 year olds.

Stephanie describes the Ninety-Nine Restaurant cuisine as American steaks, seafood, chicken, pasta dishes — just a little bit of everything. Most of the food arrives frozen; the rib-eye and haddock arrive fresh. Not much of the fresh food is bought locally; most come from the Ninety-Nine Commissary. Their markup is 66 percent on most of their food items.

They have not really adjusted prices because of competition. This is because the prices are done on the corporate level. They do some price tiers based on different regions. Stephanie says the best way for them to keep their costs down is by following a declining balance budget.

Customers of the Ninety-Nine Restaurant sometimes receive coupons in advertisements. The advertisements are mailed to homes in the area twice a year. They do not reward frequent diners. When it comes to customers being dissatisfied with their service, food, or atmosphere, Stephanie says they do the following to satisfy them:

"Get them what they want as far as food, and if they cannot be satisfied, we don't let them pay for their meal. As far as service, ensure that you apologize and make it a point to give them a gift card or free appetizer card to return on a future visit and have them ask for you (or another manager) when they

come back in — and be sure they have a wonderful visit. As far as atmosphere, change the television station or the air conditioning to make them happy unless it is not feasible."

When it comes to her employees, Stephanie says the most important trait she looks for in her wait staff is friendliness, a nice smile, and a good attitude. The managers in her store are required to cook at least one shift every two weeks to keep them up on the specs and help keep a good relationship with the kitchen staff. They do have a host/hostess, but they do not have any managerial duties over the other staff. Stephanie says they are the most inexperienced in the restaurant. The employees are required to wear a uniform shirt and black or khaki pants. They do not require the men to wear ties.

To evaluate the kitchen staff, they have semi-annual reviews that allow the managers to choose a specific measurement of specific categories of performance (for example, needs improvement, meets expectations, or exceeds expectation). The wait staff is also reviewed in the same manner, but with daily and weekly audits done as well.

To reduce accidents, they follow the safety procedures and also have a safety committee. When there are staff arguments or troubles, management will mediate between the parties involved and make decisions, trying to squash the problem before it goes too far.

They do hire outside help for things like laundry, cleaning, baking, and accounting. They do use a computer to keep their records. The system polls automatically overnight. The kitchen does have 99 percent of all the equipment it needs, unless something happens to break. They wash dishes using a machine with industrial strength sanitizers.

Stephanie says Ninety-Nine "is getting there" as far as fulfilling the dream of where it should be. If she had to do it all over again, she said she would.

Gina Marie Onorato

Company	Haro Tapas & Pintxos
Address	2436 S. Oakley Chicago, IL 60608
Role in Company	Head Chef and Manager
E-mail	chefginamarie@aol.com
Web site	**harotapas.com**
Phone	773-329-5515

Background

Chef Gina Marie Onorato is currently the Head Chef and General Manager of HARO (Tapas y Pintxos). She is one of HARO's original founding chefs and has been with the restaurant since their initial opening.

Chef Gina Marie's passion for cooking began at a very young age. Her family owned and operated an Italian restaurant in rural Southwest Illinois. Throughout her teens, she spent a lot of time working in the family business and soon realized her affinity for cooking. Her enthusiasm led her to The Cooking and Hospitality Institute of Chicago. There, she successfully completed the Le Cordon Bleu program and graduated with a degree in Culinary and a second degree in Pastry & Baking.

While attending school, she worked as a personal chef, servicing a clientele list of ten. In January 2006, she joined HARO as assistant chef. Three months later, she was promoted to her current role and responsibilities. Chef Gina Marie is no stranger to Spanish culture and is very acquainted with Spanish cuisine. Working alongside owner Javier Haro, her knowledge of Spanish cuisine has grown tremendously. She has helped create an innovative and authentic Spanish menu, with dish influences originating from the Basque and Catalan regions of Spain. Seeking first-hand experience of Spanish culture and cuisine, Chef Gina Marie traveled to Spain in 2007.

Originally from Chicago, Chef Gina Marie's family stems from a long line of law enforcement agents. Her mother, Victoria Onorato, and many of her aunts and uncles are all members of the Chicago Police Department. She has two brothers, Michael and Frank. Chef Gina Marie currently resides in the "Heart of Chicago," otherwise known as the Original Little Italy neighborhood. Her hobbies include traveling, summer sports, and reading.

Career

Gina has been in the restaurant industry for over 5 years and in restaurant management for a year and half. Her first job was in the hospitality field in a family restaurant. She decided to become a restaurant manager because she was working as the head chef in a small restaurant; becoming manager was one of the responsibilities that came with the position. She does not own the restaurant but manages eight employees at HARO's.

Her ideal employee possesses wit, charm, dependability, and a strong work ethic. The quality Gina believes she possesses that makes her a good manager is being perceptive of everyone's position at HARO's because, at one point or another, she has worked in those positions herself.

"I believe it takes patience and understanding to deal with employees and a good sense of decorum to offer to the customers to be a good manager."

Something unique Gina does in managing her employees is leading by example by aiding them in their daily duties. Her specific management style includes setting expectations about all the positions in the restaurant and educating her employees about the cultural distinctiveness of the food, wine, and social nature that sets HARO's apart.

"Because knowledge is best shared."

When she first started in her management career, Gina wishes someone had given her the advice to never expect her employees to possess the same work ethic as hers and to be able to uncover a person's weaknesses in order to work through that weakness. One of the toughest lessons Gina has had to learn in her management career thus far is how employees take advantage of the generosities the upper management team offers.

"You need to able to adjust to everyone's mood, every day."

So far in her career Gina has been highly recognized by two key media stations in Chicago (WTT 11 and 190 North) and acknowledged in many written news media. In the next five or ten years she would like to further her education in the food industry and psychology.

A major change Gina managed to implement was re-organizing the infrastructure of HARO's by adding new and fresh team members so they were able to adjust to the restaurant's growing success.

"Nothing is 100 percent successful; therefore, as a manager, it is a daily task to establish the greatest working environment."

A Little Restaurant Information

HARO's serves authentic Spanish tapas and pintxos that Gina says are unique beyond compare. The restaurant is open Tuesday through Thursday from 5 p.m. to 11 p.m., Fridays and Saturdays from 5 p.m. to 1 a.m., and is closed on Sundays and Mondays. They are also open for lunch during the summertime, and they do cater as well. Their busiest time is from 6 p.m. to 9 p.m., and they do accept reservations. Bouncers are not required, but they do have valet parking available. Alcohol is served at the restaurant, and it is important to the business.

All ages seem to enjoy the restaurant, and Gina says the distinctive tapas and pintxos, extensive wine list, and unusual cocktail menu are what set HARO's apart and help to draw in their clientele. They also have a Spanish guitarist and live flamenco dancing. Gina believes that colors affect appetite since "our eyes eat before our mouths do."

Twenty percent of the foods for the restaurant arrive frozen and 80 percent arrive fresh. They do purchase their fresh foods locally. They have never had to adjust prices because of their competition before. They use a computer to keep their daily records and hire outside professionals for some of the restaurant's needs. The kitchen has all the equipment it needs, and dishes are washed by a "human dishwasher."

Customer checks only include gratuity when they are in parties of six or more. They do offer coupons in their advertising, as well as awarding their frequent customers. When a customer is unhappy with the service, food, or atmosphere, Gina will apologize for any dissatisfaction in their experience and inquire about the misunderstanding to assure the best overall quality of service.

"No single dilemma is greater than the other."

The most important traits Gina looks for in her wait staff are personality and dependability. She has to step in for every position on a daily basis and is also the hostess for HARO's. The staff is required to follow a dress code, but the men do not have to wear ties. She does use flex scheduling for her employees. To evaluate the wait staff Gina looks at their sales. Her kitchen staff is evaluated by the productivity, time management skills, and their quality control. When a problem arises among her staff, Gina hears out both sides and tries to arrive at a conclusion that is satisfying to both parties.

Gina says HARO's has not yet fulfilled its dream of what it should be because, with every goal they accomplish, two more arise in its place. When asked if she had it to all over again would she, Gina said yes.

"Like with any family, some days are good and some are bad and I would like to walk away. But, by keeping in mind that with the relationships formed here, the good days outweigh the bad as often as they may."

Advice Tidbits

"Do not allow the title of "manager" to get to your head; be a part of the staff and not above it."

Daniel J. Pace

Company	Trattoria Bella
Address	6 Radcliffe Drive
	Moosic, PA 18507
Role in Company	President / Owner
E-mail	tbella@trattoriabella.com
Web site	**www.trattoriabella.com**
Phone	570-961-2250
Fax	570-341-5241

Dan and Leane (Owners)

Background

Daniel Pace has been in the restaurant industry for five years, in management for twenty years, and in restaurant management for four years. Besides Trattoria Bella he worked in pizza and steak establishments. One of his first jobs in the hospitality industry was cooking steaks for a steak house in Columbus, Ohio. The reason for his decision to become a restaurant owner, in his own words, was:

"I grew up in an Italian family. I've been around home cooked meals my entire life as a child. Homemade pastas, fresh-made sauces, and Italian meats hanging from a dirt basement are memories that will never be erased from my childhood."

Career

Daniel owns his own restaurant, Trattoria Bella, along with his sister Leane. Here he manages 20 full- and part-time employees. He believes a good manager in the restaurant industry needs to be firm.

"It's a business where you don't have much to control outside of cost of goods and labor from the financial side and quality and consistency from the operating side. Competition is fierce, so you want to put out a good quality product with consistency at all times. That product needs to be analyzed from a cost point to be sure your return is there and the portion needs to be correct at all times."

As far as his own qualities he believes help his management career, because he is a "charts and numbers person," he likes to compare how his restaurant is doing compared to others. Oftentimes he will post information on the industry trends for his staff to review.

"I put up our own performance measurement, such as wine and dessert sales by server, month-to-month comparisons, and our controllable expenses versus

industry standards. I believe it's important to not only show negative feedback but also to reward positive feedback. All throughout the restaurant, on server and kitchen boards, you'll find feedback forms on what our guests thought about their dining experience. Any negative forms are usually followed with corrective actions to prevent that from happening again. The fixes are usually simple for us, such as changing a button in the POS, or we may have a quality issue where we need to bring a purveyor in for a product that's not meeting our quality standards. It can also be a problem where we as management need to focus on more, for example, training. Positive feedback is also posted up for all to see. It's a good feeling when you know people appreciated everything that was done for them and that things are working."

Some qualities that his ideal employee possesses are knowledge of the field and an eye for detail and balance in the dining room, along with excellent manners.

"The culinary staff needs the eye as well; chefs need to be perfectionists. A plate can look okay and a plate can look great. People eat with their eye before they eat with their mouths."

When it comes to his specific management style, Daniel says he does a good job at drawing the line.

"It's a soap opera industry — a good manager needs to let their employees know that there is a time for fun and a time for business (when you're in the restaurant and on the clock you better be ready to work)."

Something Daniel does that is unique in his management is once in a while taking his employees out for breakfast after a long Saturday night. By the time they have cleaned up and cleared out, it is around 12:30 a.m.

"It's a great way to discuss the night's pros and cons as a team and listen to what ways they come up with to resolve the cons. It's also a great way to encourage

both front of house and back of house communication, which many restaurants seem to lack."

One of the toughest lessons he has learned while in restaurant management is to not go into business with friends.

"Friends are friends, and they shouldn't become business partners without clear guidelines. Sometimes your friends aren't who you think they are."

The best pieces of advice Daniel was given when he first started in restaurant management were to not make friends and draw the line. The piece of advice he wishes he was given when he first started was:

"Listen to your first instincts; don't get confused — everyone will have a hundred ideas. However, they're only as good as what you want to do, since you'll be running the ship."

Daniel has been recognized in his previous jobs for best international manager for a semiconductor firm, and he has been recruited and recognized for other jobs.

"In this business, since it's my own, it's difficult. You hear from the guests on how well things run and that's all anyone can ask for. It's enough because they ultimately are the ones we are here to please."

Something Daniel is proud of that he has managed to accomplish in his career thus far was bringing an innovative style of thinking to his area. The area was a place where not many people welcomed change.

"I can remember when we were building the restaurant, rumors were wild: We were crazy, it's never going to work, what is he thinking? You just need to be aggressive; if you know what you want, you need to pursue it and never let anything stop you. I knew it could work; I knew it wouldn't be easy, but by selecting the right people and putting them in the right place you can achieve

a great deal. You can't take an auto repair technician and tell him to make a Bordelaise sauce with a red wine reduction. And you need to know your own limitations."

A major change that Daniel managed to implement had to deal with a CEC kitchen manager.

"This manager was a good chef; he was not cheap but cooked well. I look at things very black and white: I pay this much and therefore expect this much in return. Our styles were just different: I felt Mondays we should open, not him; I felt we should open for lunch, as I already had a full staff in preparing and eating their lunch, not him. I didn't mind supporting events for function for local chef chapters, which was often my labor, my utility consumption, and some of my product. I just didn't see the return on the investment. Eventually we parted ways due mainly to two different philosophies — not saying one is right or one is wrong. However, in my case, I had a business to run, and all managers need to look at restaurants as a business. Has it been a positive one? Absolutely. Since then, from a business perspective, my labor cost are down about 37 percent from where they were, my food cost has remained the same or slightly lower, my sales are up just over 7 percent, my staff is happier, both front of house and back of house get along with no personality issues, and for lunch and Mondays it's been great."

One change Daniel wants to implement is a more extensive wine list so he can show the community what great wines are available.

"The Pennsylvania Restaurant Association has done a great job in legislation allowing local restaurateurs and others to be able to purchase wine from out of state wineries. There are some great wines around the states and around the world."

Daniel's estimated 2006 sales are $1.2 million. In the next five to ten years Daniel would like to accomplish a few goals he has set for the restaurant.

These goals include increases in check averages through sales persons (wait staff) training, moving into a great wine selection, and, of course, opening more restaurants in growing metropolitan areas in order to continue to grow his staff and the Trattoria Bella name.

A Little Restaurant Information

Top (Left to Right), Billy Aruscavage – First Cook PM, Pablo Viera - First Cook AM, Dan Pace – Owner / Operator, Allison Aniska - Pantry, Kenny Caffrey – Executive Chef, Joe Dutko - Sous Chef

Bottom (Left to Right), Jennifer Walsh – Dining Room Manager, Leane Pace Owner/Catering Coordinator, Heather Kindler – Floor Captain

Trattoria Bella is open from 11 a.m. to 9 p.m. Monday thru Thursday; 11 a.m. to 10:30 p.m. Friday and Saturday; and Sunday dinner only from 1 p.m. to 10 p.m. Their busiest hour is between 6:30 p.m. and 7:30 p.m. They do accept reservations. They serve innovative Italian Food.

"It's a blend of different Mediterranean ingredients that come together to serve some of the finest dishes in Northeast Pennsylvania."

They do serve alcohol, and Daniel says that it is important to the business, not only from a sales perspective, but also for the dining experience of the guests.

Trattoria Bella does cater, both on and off the premises. Although it works well for them, Daniel does caution others about it.

"Catering is a different element in terms of staffing and food and beverage consumption."

They are a member of their local Chamber of Commerce. The age group that seems to prefer the restaurant is 35 to 45 year olds, mostly business professionals, couples, and friends. They do not have valet parking or bouncers. Daniel says the thing that sets his restaurant apart and draws in clientele is one of the most important pieces of advice he can offer.

"A restaurant, as mentioned previously, is one of the most competitive industries. There are simply so many that the competition is fierce. Having played sports all my life, I've learned two things: 1) It sucks to lose, and 2) The power of a team. In Northeastern Pennsylvania you can go anywhere and have chicken parmigiana, a dish you'll never find in Italy, but something that TV commercials and media have brainwashed the public to be Italian. You could compare chicken parmigiana at 30 different places in 30 different nights around Scranton and Wilkes-Barre, but you won't find it on the menu at Trattoria Bella. Our model is based around innovation, giving our guests something different, something unique, something they'll come back for again and again."

Trattoria Bella is different from a lot of other restaurants in the activity going on around the restaurant. Daniel says you will not find 50 television screens around the bar and dining areas.

"We believe the dining experience should be enjoyed by the atmosphere, the food, and the company. Not by everyone watching a different television, whether it's the news, the weather, or who's winning the NBA game. We do have one

television at the bar that is usually tuned to a sports event. It's a 46" Plasma television and often generates conversations for our U-Shaped bar patrons to engage in."

The restaurant has never relocated, and Daniel says he believes a good location is the key to their success. Although there has been a recent trend toward coffee shops, he says this has not affected their serving of coffee. Daniel says this is because they broke the rules again.

"We serve coffee like most restaurants do, but we serve it by the French press pot. We teamed up with a local company, Electric City Roasters, and serve our own private blend of coffee and espresso. Here again, we differentiated ourselves from all our competition. The result is a fresh brewed pot of coffee every time you order. In addition, we market our own brand of coffee and sell it in the restaurant and by the whole bean."

When asked if he believes that colors affect appetite, Daniel says that, although he has heard of that, he does not spend thousands of dollars to paint his walls a certain color in hopes the customers will come.

"We believe in the whole dining experience. They came out to get away from a busy day, busy week, or for some rest and relaxation. It's our job to ensure they enjoy their experience with us."

As for the food in Trattoria Bella, they hardly ever receive anything frozen (just ice cream and a limited amount of fryer foods). Besides that, it all comes fresh. They clean it, trim it, prep it, and get it ready for consumption.

"Being an independent, we buy locally as much as possible, and we market it. We are local, and we support the locals."

Daniel describes the cuisine at Trattoria Bella as fresh and creative.

"While we offer some local favorites we tend to kick it up a notch. A bit more out of the normal, as too many restaurants today buy frozen products pumped with sodium to preserve them to have a shelf life of almost forever. We choose to work a bit harder; deliveries come four times a week. Preparation is done daily and sometimes on the spot."

The target food cost is 30 percent, but this will vary depending on profit margin and what the market will digest. Daniel has never adjusted prices due to the competition, as he says they serve a quality product. Although he knows what the competition does, he leads and lets them follow. To keep costs down, Daniel says to order frequently and control waste.

"We make all our stocks and soups; they change frequently. We use what we can for house specialties, and we are creative in the menu planning to ensure cross utilization of items."

With his customers, Daniel says it is important to remember that mistakes happen.

"If it's a problem with service, we try to get it resolved immediately. This can be changing a server with another person or just overseeing it for the rest of the dining experience. With food, again we're fair — mistakes happen, fortunately not often. If someone orders a steak medium rare and it's overcooked we are glad to exchange it for another. You ordered what you wanted, and we'll make sure you get it that way. In some instances, however, we draw the line. We add a lot of seasoning to our stocks and sauces. We take pride in the sauces we prefer. If you order a dish without sauce, that's the way you'll get it. In that instance you got what you wanted, complain about the way it tastes and you won't be compensated."

The checks at Trattoria Bella do not include gratuity. Daniel does not believe in it and says that he believes the wait staff should earn their tips.

"Most people are fair. I'll admit every once in a while you get a few who don't get compensated fairly but more often than not it works out."

Daniel will occasionally reward frequent diners with a drink or appetizer on the house, but keeps in mind they need to make money to give those frequent diners the quality they come to expect. He does not use coupons as he says it is a turn off to him and the staff.

"The coupon people just look for a bargain. They aren't there to enjoy the evening; they are out to see how much they can get for the least amount of money. We're there to provide the highest quality product and to run a successful business that our clientele know will be consistent each and every time. To do this you need to hire quality people, buy a quality product, and serve it with a smile. Unfortunately, you can't do that with Buy One, Get One Free coupons."

Trattoria Bella has 20 employees, both full- and part-time, as mentioned above. He does not use flex schedules. The most important quality that Daniel looks for in his wait staff is personality and maturity.

"I could care less if they have 30 years experience. We can teach them how we want things done. Personality is hard to teach; maturity is another one. I want people to care about our diners and want them to ensure they get good, respectable service."

On busy nights they have a host or hostess, but on other nights they will multitask. The bar is situated so that the bartender can greet the incoming guests and let them know that someone will be right with them.

"The most important thing one can do is acknowledge the guest and let them know you know they are there."

The host/hostess does have some managerial duties over the wait staff. They are to manage the dining room flow, know which servers can handle another table, and know when to slow it down a bit. The wait staff does have a dress code. They cannot wear dangling earrings, have no visible piercings, and are not allowed to chew gum. Their slacks are to be well-fitting and not painted on. The uniform shirts are to be tucked in and pressed. The men are not required to wear ties.

"Today, more and more people like to be casual."

Daniel has had to step in for his employees before. He says that it happens. Although he is not a chef himself, he has come to learn from the chefs at Trattoria Bella.

"They enjoy sharing their knowledge with me and also appreciate that the owner/manager isn't afraid to step in when required. A good team pulls together to get the job done. In regards to wait staff, I remember one particular night when we had some flooding around our area. My manager wanted to close due to evacuations; however, we are located near three hotels and felt that it would be a busy night. To make a long story short, we called in the reserves; I had my lovely wife come up and hostess as she often does on weekends, my son helped with dishes along with my father (as he always does), and my mother helped clear tables. We had to let most of our staff go home due to mandatory evacuations. Fortunately for me and my family we were out of the danger zone. My wife did an excellent job in informing our guests of the situation. The guests thought it was comical having the owner wait on them so it generated a lot of small talk tableside. In the end, it was a very profitable business day and everyone really enjoyed their dinners and the amusement. The best part, though, was spending the night with my son after all had left and enjoying a nice dessert on our patio with him at 1 a.m. All in a day's work."

To evaluate the kitchen staff, Daniel says they meet weekly — whether formally or in the kitchen somewhere. The items reviewed are food budgets, the coming week's functions, any product or staff issues they might have had, and how to correct or prevent them from reoccurring. To evaluate the wait staff, Daniel looks at check averages, guest feedback, appearance, and manners.

"I have a fantastic staff; sometimes corrections are needed, but, again, the "TEAM" pulls together and gets things done."

To handle staff squabbles, Daniel tries to put it in the open so he can prevent the problem as it is brewing rather than waiting for it to come to a boil.

"Often, if you're there you hear it: he said, she said. You have to realize it's always going to happen; it is human nature, and you just need to know when to put an end to it."

When it comes to the equipment in the kitchen, Daniel says they can always use more of it, but that spending needs to be controlled as well.

"Our motto is 'Adapt, Improvise, and Overcome.' We haven't failed yet."

The dishes at Trattoria Bella are cleaned by machine with a wash, rinse, and sanitizing cycle. Daniel says it is a must. He has instituted some steps to reduce accidents in his restaurant.

"All entries and bathrooms are ADA accessible, our wait staff and kitchen personnel are required to wear non-slip shoes, and any time a floor is wet the 'Caution Wet Floor' sign comes out. Spills and broken glass or china are cleaned up immediately."

Daniel hires outside companies to take care of some things. The laundry and accounting are both done by outside companies. All the other tasks (except those required for local codes and licensing) are completed in-house.

"I see some chain restaurants being cleaned by outside companies, and more

often than not they are the dirtiest places I've ever eaten in. The staff just thinks 'that's not my job.'"

Daniel does use a computer to keep the daily records of the restaurant.

"As I said, I'm a charts and numbers person. I want to know what sales are compared to alcohol, what is being comp'ed, or what voids we have and why. What are my labor and food cost percentages for a given period and what adjustments need to be made moving forward?"

When I asked Daniel if his restaurant has fulfilled his dream of what it should be, he told me it was getting there.

"A lot of long hours and long days — for both me and my wife, it's a hobby. I don't think individuals should open restaurants to make money. That's too frustrating. Look at a restaurant as a way to please your guests, enjoy the company, and watch them enjoy themselves. If you can do that the money will come, but you can't rush it."

Finally, when asked if he would do it over again, Daniel said he is already looking.

Advice Tidbits

"Restaurants are a difficult business; it's fun and can be rewarding. Be prepared to work hard; weekends are a must. If you like to go out on weekends you can still do so; however, it might be early morning and not late night. Enjoy it; watch your guests enjoy the food, the wine, and the atmosphere. That's what it's about. Tables buying other tables drinks, it's your own little way of giving back to your community. Be the best restaurant you can be and people will appreciate it."

Sue Paulson

Company	MCBP Enterprises, Inc.
	My Turn Pub
Role in Company	Partner
Web site	**www.myturnpub.com**

Background

Sue Paulson has been in the restaurant industry for six years. She has been in management for 15 years and, of those, six years in restaurant management so far. She, along with her husband, is a grill/tavern owner of My Turn Pub in Wisconsin. Besides My Turn Pub, she was also a cook in high school for Garden Gate restaurant. She decided to become a restaurant manager when partnering with her husband to fulfill his dream of owning a tavern.

Career

Sue manages five employees and says her ideal employee is reliable, energetic, friendly, and honest. She says good verbal communication and organizational skills, the ability to resolve conflicts, and the ability to think creatively to solve problems or challenges are what it takes to be a good manager. The qualities she possesses that she believes help in her management career are her good health and loads of energy, her business and accounting experience, and her communication skills training. Her specific management style focuses on quality training, process/policy documentation for staff reference, and empowering her staff to serve their customers well.

When she first started in restaurant management, Sue wishes she had been given advice on cash and inventory control. The best piece of advice she was given was to watch her staff closely for giveaways and theft of cash and products. The toughest lesson she had to learn was about customers.

"I learned to not allow a customer, who has been refused service or entry into the tavern, to return without sincere apology/explanation for behavior and payment for any damages."

A major change Sue and her husband managed to accomplish was taking the tavern, which the previous owner had operated for 35 years before them, from "an early day card party and coffee crowd to a fast, casual tavern and restaurant operation with buffet dinners for special occasions." They want to have more entertainment and music, but because of the cost and the ambivalence of their local patrons, they have not been able to guarantee a good crowd will support it.

In the next five to ten years Sue and her husband's goal is to find a person or group to take over the business for them.

A Little Restaurant Information

My Turn Pub serves fast, casual food (burgers, grilled sandwiches, appetizers, pizza, and so on). They are open from 11 a.m. to bar time. The busiest hour is from noon to 1 p.m. They do serve alcohol and say that is important to the business. They do not cater or take reservations. The main age group that seems to prefer the tavern is 25 to 60 year olds. Sue says the consistency and quality of their food served, their competent staff, and their clean and bright facility are what set the restaurant apart and draw in their customers. They have standard Wisconsin tavern offerings of TV, pool, darts, and other games.

"We have a racquetball court on the second level. The public ATV riding

trail brings in many customers, especially from out-of-town, and from the neighboring states of Iowa and Illinois."

If a customer is unhappy with the food Sue will offer a replacement or substitution at no charge to the customer. They do not reward their frequent diners or offer any coupons in their advertising.

Sue describes the cuisine as fast casual. She says about 50 percent of the food is frozen and 50 percent is fresh. She does buy the fresh food locally. She has never adjusted the prices at the tavern because of competition. Her markup is 100 percent. She has found the best way to keep costs down is through inventory control, minimizing waste and spoilage, and using automated cooking equipment to reduce the staffing requirements. She uses a computer to keep daily records and does not hire out for any of the other duties. The dishes are washed by hand and then put through a machine cycle.

The most important trait Sue looks for in her wait staff is their availability for scheduling, stability for reliability, and experience or an eagerness to learn. She has had to step in for her employees before. They do not have a host or hostess or a need for bouncers. The employees are not required to wear a certain uniform, as there is no dress code for the staff. Sue does use flex scheduling. She evaluates the staff informally by frequent communication on what is going well or where improvements may be needed or desired. Sue says she uses communication and cause analysis to eliminate any conflict among her staff.

Advice Tidbits

"Keep in mind you must be energetic and flexible. Your personal life is often sacrificed when you are understaffed or have an unexpected busy period in the operation."

Paul Petrulis

Company	The Union League Club of Chicago
Address	65 West Jackson Blvd, Suite 911
	Chicago, IL 60604
Role in Company	Food and Beverage Director
E-mail	petrulis@ulcc.org
Web site	**www.ulcc.org**
Phone	312-427-7800 ext. 430

UNION LEAGUE CLUB OF CHICAGO

Background

Paul Petrulis has been in the restaurant industry for 9 years and in management for 8 of those years. Besides his current position as the food and beverage director of The Union League Club of Chicago, he has also worked for the Signature Room at the 95th, Carmine's, and Carlucci (all places in Chicago). His first job in the hospitality industry was as a bartender. He decided to become a manager because of pride and wanting to make decisions.

"Putting my 'fingerprint' on a facility and staff."

Career

As the Food and Beverage Director at The Union League Club of Chicago, Paul currently manages 75 employees. Previously his number of employees managed has been at 180. Paul's annual sales for 2006 are estimated to be $8 million. His ideal employee possesses punctuality, a sense of humbleness, the desire to work, and the ability to be helpful to others.

Paul believes it takes the ability to relate to your employees as humans and not employees that makes someone a good manager. He also believes the ability to listen and to stay committed when things go wrong are also necessary. He believes his commitment to the job, his strong sense of humility, and his ability to listen and communicate at the human level are the qualities he possesses that help in his management career. His specific management style includes working with the staff.

"Give them enough 'rope' to hang themselves, then be firm. Always let the staff know where you stand on issues and remain consistent."

Something Paul does that is unique to other managers is letting his staff help in developing training sessions and allowing them input on changes. He says it makes transitions much easier for his employees when they are the ones helping create the change.

The toughest lesson Paul had to learn when he first started in management was to not be friends with the staff on a personal level. He says that it will eventually hurt a manager's objectivity. When he first started in management he wishes someone would have told him to take baby steps, get to know his facility and staff, and that sweeping changes would be difficult to manage effectively. The best advice he was given when he first started was that he would work longer than he would think and that he would love his career.

One thing Paul managed to do in his career that he has been proud of was helping with the reduction in liquor costs in every facility through training and people management. Some changes he has managed to implement during his career thus far has been a complete overhaul of the training programs and expectations at his current facility.

"Change was needed because the activities were outdated and did not match the ambience of the facility. The change has been positive thus far."

A change Paul would like to implement, but has yet to do so far, is having an increased wine presence in both sales and knowledge of his staff. He has not had enough time to get it started, but he is working on this in pieces.

In five years Paul's goal is to be the General Manager of a country club. In ten years his goal is to still be GM of a country club with improving expectations of himself and membership.

A Little Restaurant Information

The Union League Club of Chicago serves fine dining American cuisine. The restaurant serves breakfast from 6 a.m. to 11 a.m., lunch from 11 a.m. to 3:30 p.m., and dinner from 3:30 p.m. to 9 p.m. Room service is offered during all these times as well. They also have a full bar from 11 a.m. to 1 a.m. daily. The busiest time for the restaurant is at noon for lunch. They do serve alcohol and say it is important to the business. They do occasionally do some catering as well. Because they are a private club, Paul says the expectations in their product and service is higher than most freestanding facilities.

"The private club is housed in a 25-story building that includes a full athletic facility, basketball court, swimming pool, 200-room hotel, 28 different meeting rooms, and banquet space to accommodate up to 400 in a single room. There are three restaurants in the building, as well as a pool table in the bar area."

They do take reservations and have valet parking. The average age of their members is 56.2 years old. They are also active in their community.

"The Club is very active in Boys & Girls Clubs, civic and arts programs, as well as the staples of Chambers of Commerce, et cetera."

They use 10 percent frozen foods and 90 percent fresh. They try as best they can to buy their fresh foods locally. Although they are American cuisine, their chefs change the daily specials to their strength (French, Cuban, Italian, and so forth). Their markup is around 100 to 150 percent.

They do not reward frequent diners or offer coupons in their advertising. When they have a customer who is unhappy with some aspect of their visit, Paul says it depends on the situation how they will handle it.

"Usually we remove items from the bill or give the member something on the house for their inconvenience."

When it comes to his staff, Paul does use flex scheduling. The most important trait he looks for in his wait staff is that they have a personality. He has had to step in for all his employees' positions at one time or another. They do have a host/hostess, but they do not have any managerial duties over the staff. They do not need bouncers. They do require a dress code be followed. The men are only required to wear ties on a predetermined formal occasion.

Every six months the kitchen staff is evaluated based on their quality of food, presentation, willingness to stop production of an inferior product, the cleanliness of their work station, punctuality, and more. The wait staff is evaluated based on their quality of service steps, consistency of steps, willingness to stop production of an inferior product, product knowledge, punctuality, and more. How he handles staff squabbles depends on the situation.

"If it is between two staff members, you put them both in the same room and let them talk it out with the manager. It is amazing how things get all twisted out of shape when the people actually sit down to talk about it, rather than listen to the rumor-mill."

Paul does hire an outside company for sharpening of their knives. They use a computer to keep all daily records of the Club. The kitchen does have all the equipment needed, and dishes are washed by hand and then by machine with typical Ecolab cleaning products. To help reduce accidents in the Club, they have created a safety committee, require non-slip shoes be worn, and do safety training seminars, as well as other steps.

The Club has had to reduce their costs due to competition. Gratuity is included on guest's checks. Paul finds the best way to save on costs is to get the staff to understand what they are supposed to do, train them, and then keep a constant, trained eye on them.

Paul says, for the most part, the restaurant has fulfilled the dream of what it should be. He says if he had it all to do all over again, there would be no question — he would.

Advice Tidbits

"Even though turnover is inevitable, hire better people than you need and always have some staff ready to go. Try not to hire people just because you need a body — plan ahead as best you can."

Elin Trousdale

Company	Le Bistro
Address	4626 North Federal Highway
	Lighthouse Point, Florida 33064
Role in Company	Owner / Manager
E-mail	andyelin@bellsouth.net
Web site	**www.lebistrorestaurant.com**
Phone	954-946-9240

Andy, Elin, and Chandler Trousdale, Le Bistro Restaurant

Background

Elin Trousdale graduated Sullivan County School of Hospitality Management & Culinary in 1979. She worked at several New York City Hotels until she decided the only way she could make real money was to be a General Manager of a hotel. She decided that would take too long and that she would have to work way too many hours for someone else. With that in mind, she left the industry and went into real estate. Fifteen years later she married a chef and invested money she had earned in her real estate career with him to purchase their restaurant. She came full circle by chance and learned some great skills from her earlier careers in cost control, catering, public relations, and real estate to run their business. Elin has been in the restaurant industry for six years now and in management for all six years.

Career

Elin, along with her husband Andy, own Le Bistro in Florida. Elin manages three to six employees and says her ideal employee is friendly, reliable, smart, conscientious, loyal, and honest. She believes knowledge, diplomacy, delegation, and camaraderie are what it takes to make a good manager. The qualities she possesses that she believes help in her management career are her ability to read people, sharing in the workload, treating employees fairly, ironing out difficulties, admitting mistakes, allowing others to utilize their talents, and not being bossy. Her management style is laid back unless it becomes necessary to be otherwise. Something unique about her management is the way she treats everyone the same.

The toughest lesson Elin has learned while in management has been that trust is to be earned and not just assumed. The one piece of advice she wishes she was given when she first started in management was to try to get to know your new employee's personality and dependability first before fully investing in training them.

Elin was able to help transform the early bird restaurant they purchased into a fine dining establishment. Some changes she was able to implement involved the décor, music, and wine list. Something she would like to change is to move the location of the restaurant because she says it is not great for fine dining.

A Little Restaurant Information

Le Bistro serves French-based international and spa cuisine. It is open from 5 p.m. to 10 p.m. Their busiest time begins at 7:30 p.m., and they do accept reservations. They serve wine and beer and say that alcohol is very important to their business. They also do catering. The fine dining and friendly attitude are what set Le Bistro apart, according to Elin. They are a member of their local Chamber of Commerce. The age group that seems to prefer Le Bistro the most is 40 to 60 year olds.

Elin describes the cuisine at Le Bistro as great. One hundred percent of the food arrives fresh. Much of it is purchased from local vendors. They continually adjust their prices based upon cost of goods and to keep in line with the market. Elin says the best way to keep costs down is to keep a tight watch on everything, do as much as possible on your own, control buying, and make everything in house. She does hire outside companies for some of the work of the restaurant (laundry, repairs) and uses a computer to keep all the daily records of the business. The kitchen has all the equipment it needs, and the dishes are done by machine. They have had no accidents.

Le Bistro does reward its frequent diners by treating them to wine/food, gift certificates. They do not put coupons in advertisements. Although it rarely happens that a customer is not pleased with the service or food, Elin says that you cannot please everyone.

"It depends what the circumstances are — some people fabricate stories to get

something for free. We analyze each and every circumstance and then decide what course of action to take."

When it comes to her staff, Elin says the most important trait she looks for is for their appearance to be clean and professional, as well as for them to be nice and not back talk. Elin has had to step in for her employees before in the kitchen and as a waitress. She also acts as the hostess for Le Bistro. She does have a dress code for her staff, which includes black dress pants/skirts and black or white dress shirts, but she does not require the men to wear a tie. She does not use flex scheduling.

Elin evaluates the kitchen staff by seeing how they pay attention to what they are doing, as well as their punctuality. To evaluate her wait staff, she will closely watch them as they do their duties. To handle staff squabbles, Elin will talk to each party involved and then have them talk to each other.

Elin says Le Bistro has fulfilled her dreams of what it should be. When asked if she had to do it all over again would she, Elin said maybe.

"It's fun and it's mine with my husband. I just wish we had more free time to travel."

Advice Tidbits

"Always have backup staff to call on!"

Joseff A. VanHorn

Company	Celebration Banquets and Catering & Chicago's Deep Dish 'N Dogs (Restaurant)
Address	2121 Celebration Dr. Grand Rapids, MI 49519
Role in Company	General Manager of Food and Beverage
E-mail	jvanhorn@celebrationcinema.com
Web site	**www.celebrationbanquets.com**
Phone	616-447-4200 ext. 1355
Fax	616-447-4201

Background

Joseff A. VanHorn has been in the restaurant industry for 20 years, since he was 16 years old. He has been in management for 14 years, with 10 of those in restaurant management. Besides his current restaurant he has also worked in fine dining, family casual, mom-and-pop restaurants, and major chains. His first job in the hospitality industry was at the age of 15 at Midway Motor Lodge, where he worked as banquet setup, busboy, and room service. He decided to get into restaurant management because he was inspired by the people he worked for and wanted the challenge.

Career

Joseff manages 50 employees and says his ideal employee is an honest people person who is willing to learn. He believes that leading by example and showing your employees that you are not above rolling up your sleeves and jumping in wherever needed is what it takes to be a good manager. That includes doing dishes, busing tables, and anything else that needs attention. Joseff is a systems person and is an organizer, motivator, and dedicated to succeeding in everything he does. He says all these qualities are what help him in his management career. His specific management style is leading by example.

"The lead by example, please-and-thank-you manager style, empowering the

right people in the right places doing the right things. I reward success and hold everyone accountable to abide by all company rules and regulations."

Something unique he does with his management is listening to his employees' ideas and using them to better his operation. The toughest lesson he has learned in his management career has been to not play favorites. The best advice he was given when he started in restaurant management was to stay focused on the end result.

"If you want to be a GM, put in your time and do the best you can at everything you do. If you are a server, be the BEST server; if you are a dishwasher, be the BEST dishwasher. Those people who are/will be successful will naturally gravitate to the top."

He wishes that he had been told to stay focused on his career and balance his home life when he first started in restaurant management.

"Quality of life is more important than any restaurant job you may have. If the company is worth its salt, they will ensure their employees have the best quality of life possible."

Joseff has been recognized as a leader in his community. He believes that giving back and being part of the community is very important. He has operated the number one store in some of the chains he worked for.

"Everywhere I go I help drive sales higher and improve their systems. I have successfully started businesses from scratch and watched them flourish."

A change that Joseff has managed to implement has been to be an advocate for the people, creating fairness for all while bridging the gap between his staff and the corporate office. In the coming years, his goals are to drive his business to be number one in the industry. He would also love to strike out on his own when the timing is right.

A Little Restaurant Information

Employee Meeting – October 1, 2006

Chicago's Deep Dish 'N Dogs serves Chicago style pasta, pizza, hot dogs, and salads. Celebration caters steaks, seafood, chicken, and more. Deep Dish 'N Dogs is open from 11 a.m. to 10 p.m. Monday through Thursday, 11 a.m. to 11 p.m. on Friday and Saturday, and 11 a.m. to 9 p.m. on

Sunday. Although lunch is busy, their busiest times are weekend nights from 6 p.m. to 9 p.m. They serve beer and wine, and he says it is a nice amenity. He uses red and gold in the restaurant theme and says that he does believe colors affect appetite. The restaurant is geared toward family dining and attracts all ages.

They are a member of the Grand Rapids Chamber of Commerce and West Michigan Hispanic Chamber of Commerce. Joseff says having the Chicago style cuisine in Grand Rapids (being three hours from Chicago) is what sets the restaurant apart and draws in customers. They just added televisions so customers can see sports games. They do not have valet parking or take reservations.

Joseff describes the cuisine as cutting edge, Chicago style, and Italian. They use 90 percent fresh foods and 10 percent frozen foods. The fresh foods are bought locally whenever possible.

They do reward their frequent diners (with such things as punch cards where you buy four and get the fifth one free, buy one get one, and business card drawings for free lunches), and they offer coupons in advertising as well. Joseff says they do whatever they can within their means to make an unsatisfied guest happy again.

"If the food is wrong we will make it right. If they call, we will send them a letter to entice them to come back and try us again."

On parties of eight or more, their checks include gratuity. They have had to adjust their prices due to the competition before — they actually had to increase it. Joseff says the best way to keep costs down is by controlling the things that can be controlled.

"Labor and food cost can make you or break you."

The most important quality Joseff looks for in his staff is that they are outgoing and friendly. He evaluates his kitchen staff by their cleanliness, presentation, attendance, and attitude. His wait staff is evaluated by their cleanliness, organization, attendance, and attitude. He does use flex scheduling. There is no need for bouncers at the restaurant. They do have a host/hostess. This person also helps do voids and handles cash. He sometimes has had to step in for an employee once in a while.

"I will support them all the best way I can. I will not let them go down in flames."

There is a dress code for the staff, but the men are not required to wear ties. The restaurant dress code changes with the seasons. During the summer they wear black polo shirts and khakis. They do have the option of wearing shorts as long as they are approved. They also wear a black apron. During the winter the servers wear black long sleeve shirts, black pants, and a black apron. The banquet staff wears white shirts, black pants, and a black vest that is provided for them and that has the logo on the chest. The more formal events require the banquet staff to wear all black ties. For outdoor catering they wear white polo shirts and khaki pants or shorts.

Joseff will listen to both sides when there is a staff squabble. He will help them work it out, but if the problem becomes too great, he will terminate an employee.

A low-temp dish machine washes the dishes in the restaurant. They do have a lot of make-do equipment for the little things in the kitchen. To reduce accidents, they keep mats down on the floor when the weather is bad, post signs that caution of wet floors, and train the staff to clean spills up immediately. A computer is used to keep all daily records of the business, and he does sometimes have to hire outside companies for some jobs.

"I do have a knife company sharpen our knives, and I will never clean my own

kitchen towels again. It is so nice to not have to clean all the grease and be able to send the dirty towels and aprons to someone else."

When asked if he had it to all over again would he, Joseff said yes. He says, as long as if the restaurant has fulfilled the dream of what it should be, that he cannot settle.

"There is always a better, faster way, and I am always seeking cutting edge cuisine to stay steps above the competition."

Advice Tidbits

"Remember that the restaurant business for most is a stepping stone in their life. Some work to pay their way through school and some just work in the restaurant business until 'they get a real job.' If I had a nickel for every time I have heard that I'd be rich.

"Make the best of your staff. Every customer leaves happy no matter what, abide by your company rules and regulations, and be an advocate for your staff. There is nothing more gratifying than hiring a brand new employee out of high school with no experience, giving them the tools they need to be successful, and watching them mature through life. Most will leave and try other things, some will leave and keep trying to come back, and if you're real they will never forget their time with your facility."

Carolyn Wells

Company	St. Bernard's School
Address	4 East 98th St. New York City, NY 10129
Role in Company	Chef / Manager
E-mail	wellsc690@aol.com
Web site	**saintbernards.org**
Phone	212-289-7879
Fax	212-010-6628

Background

Carolyn Wells has been in the food service industry since 1983 and in management for about 15 years. She worked for a number of New York City restaurants, as well as corporate catering facilities. Her first hospitality job was as a waitress. In 1983, Carolyn moved to France to study cooking and worked on hotel barges in Burgundy. She is a self-taught professional.

Career

Carolyn runs the school cafeteria at St. Bernard's school in New York City. The company she works for, Cater To You, serves six other private schools in New York. She manages five employees at St. Bernard's. In her opinion, the ideal employee has a positive attitude and initiative, the most important factors for success in the workplace.

She believes a good manager needs patience, firmness, and fairness. Carolyn is even-tempered, hands on, flexible, and creative. She tries to keep a cool head under pressure. Organization is of utmost importance, as well as creating an atmosphere of mutual respect.

One tough lesson she learned was to avoid being "too nice."

"If you only worry about pleasing others and having them like you, it may not help you in getting the job done."

Carolyn is responsible for special events at the school. Some of them include Japan Day and a Roman banquet for 400 children and 450 adults. She feels that St. Bernard's has been a very supportive atmosphere and has helped her grow professionally. She sets high standards and much is expected of her.

Carolyn is trying to make changes in the food by introducing healthier choices and more local produce. High fructose sweets and overly processed food have been eliminated. She hopes to use only organic meats soon.

Her goal in the next five years is to promote healthy eating in schools and to become more of an executive chef and less of a hands-on cook.

A Little Restaurant Information

St. Bernard's serves simple, home cooked food, lunch for approximately 500 every day. The students love pizza, pasta, BBQ, Asian food, and ice cream especially. The children can choose from an extensive salad bar or a hot line. Most of the products come from Sysco Food Company.

The employees are required to wear hair restraints and dress professionally. The school is inspected every year by the New York City Department of Health.

Dishes are sanitized, stress mats cover the floors, and hand washing signs are posted. Carolyn uses food well to avoid waste and to stay within the budget.

Although Carolyn loves food and cooking, she admits it is a very difficult profession and probably would have become a French teacher if she had it to do over again.

Advice Tidbits

"Keep a cool head, learn how to multitask, and try to have fun in a stressful environment."

Gastone A. Zampieri

Address	P.O. Box 1853
	Belize City, Belize,
	Central America
Role in Company	Retired Restaurant Manager
E-mail	giotto1@msn.com

Background

Gastone A. Zampieri was born in Padova, Italy. He received his diploma from the Professional Hotel Training Institute in Padova, Italy in 1977 and has certificates from The National Restaurant Association, Banquet, Kitchen Management, Italian Sommelier Society, German Wine Society, and Seagram's Hospitality. He took his Master Sommelier first course in 1994 and Master of Wine Course in 1991. He was certified as Wine Specialist in 2003 by the Society of Wine Educators. He speaks fluent Italian and English, is proficient in French and Spanish, and has working knowledge of German. He was in the restaurant industry for 28 years in both Europe and the United States. He was in management for 24 years and in restaurant management for 18 of those years.

Gastone started in the hospitality field at the age of 14 when he worked in a small bar in a tiny village outside of Padua, Italy. He has worked for many other restaurants in Washington, D.C., and throughout Europe throughout his career and said he wanted to become a restaurant manager because he had knowledge of the work and the ability to deal with different people in a different manner. He is married and is now retired, but the last restaurant he managed was La Colline restaurant in Washington, D.C.

Career

Gastone never owned his own restaurant, but the largest number of employees he managed was 24. His ideal employee possesses a willingness to learn, is happy to be at work even when the world outside is falling, maintains high standards, is able to understand customer needs, and can be a team player.

He believes it takes many things to be a good manager, including patience, good communication (which goes two ways — listening to what you are told and demonstrating your understanding), being able to buffer between owners who pay you and the workers who maintain your standards, and maintaining a fair attitude because at work it is business and outside is friendship.

"Therefore, manage with a punch with a velvet glove."

Gastone believes his management skills include patience, fear, and all the other items mentioned above. In addition, he is also able to add his knowledge of food and wine and always is interested in learning something new everyday. His specific management style is just being himself. Something unique he would do in managing his employees was to listen and make them feel that he was there and available at any moment during the work hours.

The toughest lesson Gastone learned in his career was that the customer is not always right, but they are the ones who pay the bill. When he first started in management he wishes someone had told him to remember that he is the "orchestra's director."

"You are alone in front of a lot of people and everything has to go smooth."

Some things Gastone did in his career were to open the first champagne bar in D.C., opening restaurants, and his wine achievements. He also had the opportunity to be at the right place at the right time when President George H.W. Bush came for dinner after the "I Ricchi" restaurant he worked at in D.C. was open for two months. He is very proud of the fact that he made decisions in his career that brought him from working in a bar to working in first class, five star hotels and restaurants around the world.

Because Gastone is retired he does not really have any business plans in the next five or ten years but does say that the restaurant industry is a business where you can make plans.

"Many times the plans will change often and sometimes out of your hands because we never know where opportunity is next."

Gastone would not make any major changes immediately when starting at a restaurant. He believes the saying "If it is not broken do not fix it" is always valid. After a short watching period at any restaurant that he worked at he wanted to have everything clear from job description to individual duty before, during, and after the service.

"The result was positive, and the reason was that the staff was always involved; therefore, upon agreement during final meeting over the changes, every one was clear on what to do."

A Little Restaurant Information

(This information is about the last restaurant Gastone worked for and his experience there — La Colline Restaurant in Washington, D.C.)

Gastone was Maitre d'hotel of La Colline Restaurant from August 1990 to October 1999. The restaurant was closed after 25 years of operation. It was sold but is re-opening soon. He was responsible for supervising and maintaining dining room operations. There, he used to serve classical French food. The restaurant was open for breakfast, lunch, and dinner. They served alcohol, as it was an important aspect to the business. They did not cater but did accept reservations.

Their ability to make the customers feel welcome all the time as if each visit was their first was what set apart the restaurant and drew in its clientele. Because many of the patrons at the restaurant were politicians, their best feature was having the television always on C-Span.

"We used to aim to the best people without any particular age in mind. In fact, parents brought their children. Their children would then be the next customer.

In this manner we could maintain our clientele and groom clientele for the future."

La Colline was committed to having the freshest food and tried to produce as much in house as possible. When it was possible they did purchase their fresh foods from local vendors. They never had to adjust their pricing because of their competition and found the best way to keep costs down was to try not to make many mistakes and control everything. Customer checks did not include gratuity.

The recent trend toward coffee shops has now more than before affected the serving of coffee because that is the last memory of the customer. Gastone says it is sometimes a good idea to offer coupons in advertising, but in most cases it is costly and the return does not pay off. In a situation in which the customer is dissatisfied with everything there was not much he could do, so it was not good to invite them back.

"If I knew the restaurant was in a transaction time, I would try to suggest the customer come back. For me it is a very fine line, and it is not always worth it to give away food or an invitation for dinner. Yes, I will listen and be considerate about the problem and I would take action accordingly."

When it comes to wait staff, the most important trait Gastone would look for was the ability to be attentive but not intrusive with their customer service. He often had to step in for members of his staff.

"In the restaurant business it is a daily routine. So you need to be on the watch at any time."

They did not have a host/hostess but sometimes Gastone wished they did have one available. He does not believe the host/hostess should have any managerial duties over other members of the staff unless they are part of the management crew. At La Colline they did not require bouncers, but when he managed a night club they did, and he said that was an experience. He only used flex scheduling during the low season of the restaurant, if there was one. To evaluate his staff, Gastone would have frequent meetings with the chef and managers to evaluate all performance based on duties.

Gastone believes any well-respected establishment should require their staff to wear uniforms, but did not make the men wear ties, as casual elegant is more the trend nowadays. To handle staff squabbles he first will try to calm down the individuals and take them away from the traffic or open areas and then listen to the different stories.

"In the end the people involved will face each other in the office, and then a disciplinary decision will be made, obviously depending on the case."

They used a computer to keep the daily records of the restaurant, and the kitchen had all the equipment it needed and no make-do was necessary. To reduce accidents in the restaurant, they put up signs to make sure the staff was aware of a dangerous situation that could happen. La Colline did use outside companies for some of the professional services.

"Usually accounting is almost imperative; all others depend on the restaurant size and space. La Colline had its own laundry. The chefs knew how to sharpen their knives and lighting was one of the duties for the wait staff. For cleaning we had a person that every morning was there to vacuum, dust, and check bathrooms constantly — even during service."

Gastone said La Colline did fulfill the dream of what they wanted it to be. If he had to do it all over again, he said yes, he would, because he had a lot of fun and met a lot of people.

"The best part of all was I met my wife and had the ability to travel the world and stay long enough in different countries to understand the different types of culture."

Advice Tidbits

"Restaurant business is not a simple task. The business continues to evolve almost every year; therefore, you have to re-invent constantly; there is no time to relax for success. Just enjoy the moment because success tomorrow could already be gone. Be thankful for the recognition and continue with your guidelines for good work."

Mansoor Zia

Company	94th Squadron Restaurant
Address	5240 Paint Branch Parkway College Park, MD 20740
Role in Company	General Manager
E-mail	gmunit44@srcmail.com
Web site	**www.src.com**
Phone	301-699-9400
Fax	301-779-2305

Background

Mansoor Zia has been in the restaurant industry for 22 years and in management for 16 of those years. Besides his current position as General Manager of 94th Squadron Restaurant he has also worked at Bob's Big Boy, Rendezvous, Panavino, Julian's, and Bob Seafood, among others. His first job was not in the hospitality field, but rather was in banking. He wanted to become a restaurant manager because it is fascinating and interesting.

Career

Mansoor Zia does not own his own restaurant, but as General Manager of 94th Squadron he manages 75 employees. His ideal employee is loyal, sincere, and professional. He believes professionalism, determination, knowledge, and a desire to succeed are what it takes to be a good manager.

The qualities Mansoor Zia possesses that he says help in his management career are his experience, knowledge, professionalism, planning abilities, leadership and people skills, and his own desire to succeed. His management style is bureaucratic and democratic. Something he does that is unique when managing his employees is train, educate, and respect them, along with believing in the philosophy that people are working with him rather than for him.

The toughest lesson Mansoor Zia has learned so far is that, if you do not plan ahead, you will be in trouble. He was given good advice when he first started, telling him that he is trainable and could still be taught. He wishes when he first started in management that he had been given the advice to learn how to plan and gain confidence and knowledge.

"A reader is a leader."

In the next five or ten years Mansoor Zia would like to be in an executive corporate position, like the Vice President of Operations. He was acknowledged for his training of numerous employees, running of the Food and Beverage Department as the director of the department in the F&B director's absence, and for his reduction of food and labor costs, among others.

Some things in his career thus far that Mansoor Zia is proud of is his earning of his MBA, receiving numerous certifications, such as Certified Food and Beverage Executive (CFBE), Certified Hospitality Department Trainer (CHDT), tips instructor, and receiving Manager of the Quarter. The estimated annual sales from 2006 were $2.6 million.

A Little Restaurant Information

94th Squadron Restaurant serves all-American food, such as steaks, pasta, and seafood. They are open seven days a week. Their hours are Monday through Thursday from 11 a.m. to 10 p.m., Friday and Saturday from 11 a.m. to 11 p.m., and on Sunday from 10 a.m. to 10 p.m. Their busiest time is from 6 to 9 p.m., and they accept reservations. They do offer catering as well. They are members of their local Chamber of Commerce. They do serve alcohol and say it is important to the business. They do not have valet parking but do require bouncers.

Mansoor Zia says 94th Squadron is very thematic, which sets it apart and helps draw in its clientele. They also have forms of entertainment, such as televisions and musicians. The age group that seems to prefer the restaurant is the 35 to 55 age range.

Approximately 35 percent of the foods served at 94th Squadron arrive frozen. They purchase their fresh foods locally. Mansoor Zia says they have had to adjust their pricing before due to competition. He has found the best way to keep costs down is by following recipes, portion control, theft control, and better menu engineering.

When it comes to his employees they are required to follow a dress code, which includes the men wearing ties. There is a host/hostess, but that person does not have any managerial duties over the other staff members. Mansoor Zia does not use flex scheduling, and he has had to step in for members of his staff before.

The evaluation of the kitchen staff is generally performance-based, including their job knowledge, judgment, attitude, attendance records, safety and sanitation awareness, and productivity. The wait staff is evaluated based on their professionalism, personality, presentation, sales skills, people skills, judgment, attendance records, menu knowledge, and public relations skills.

To handle staff arguments 94th Squadron attempts to maintain a friendly atmosphere and keep communication open. Mansoor Zia tries to remain impartial, take strong action against squabbles, follow company policies and procedures, and work with the assignment of work to his employees.

Outside companies are hired for some of the professional jobs needed, such as laundry and knife sharpening. They do use a computer to keep the daily records for the restaurant. The kitchen has all the equipment needed, including the machine that the dishes are washed with. To reduce accidents in the restaurant, they follow safety policies and procedures closely, emphasize safety first principles, have regular meetings, and educate the staff to promote awareness.

For their customers, they do offer coupons and reward their frequent diners. Customer checks do not include gratuity. If a customer is unsatisfied with the food, atmosphere, or service, they will take immediate corrective action to try and satisfy the customer. They will listen, give the customer their attention as they explain the problem, and then attempt to correct the situation accordingly.

Mansoor Zia says the 94th Squadron Restaurant has not yet fulfilled the dream of what they want it to be. If he had the chance to do it all over, he said he would.

Advice Tidbits

"Plan ahead, keep an eye on abstracts/figures, have analytical skills, train your employees, be determined and confident – if you cannot control yourself you can not control others – and have strong decision-making powers."

Section

2

What These Managers Taught Us

"Restaurants are a difficult business; it's fun and can be rewarding...Be the best restaurant you can be and people will appreciate it."

~Daniel J. Pace

"Always have faith in yourself and your people."

~Michael Larey

"I believe it is critical to teach the "whys" behind the 'hows.'"

~ Kristopher Kotte

"In the end you are only as good as the team you put together."

~ Nazir N. Khamisa

"Major changes come from a series of minor ones; make the changes that are required as they come and a major one may not be required."

~ Ron Kalenuik, aka Chef K

Chapter 1

The Employees

According to The National Restaurant Association, **www.restaurant.org,** the restaurant industry employs 12.8 million people and is the largest employer besides the government. They also state that the restaurant industry is expected to add two million jobs over the next ten years and that nearly half of all adults have worked in the restaurant industry at some point during their lives. (See the chart in the appendix with more statistics from the NRA).

Hiring Employees

When hiring employees, the main goal is to find the person who is the best possible fit for the position. The participants interviewed in this book gave the following as the qualities they look for most in their employees:

- Loyal

- Sincere

- Professional

- Willingness to learn

- Happy to be at work

- Maintaining high standards

- Experience

- Eagerness

- Commitment

- Humility

- Knowledge

- Maturity

- Understanding of customer needs
- Team player
- Attentive to customers
- Ability to keep cool under pressure
- Positive attitude
- Initiative
- Honest
- Outgoing
- Friendliness
- Reliable
- Smart
- Conscientious
- Appearance
- Cleanliness
- Energetic
- Availability
- Ability to work independently
- Humor
- Self-respect
- Flexibility
- Ability to think for themselves

- Stability
- An eye for detail
- Charisma
- Charm
- Strong work ethic
- Caring
- Wit
- Dependability
- Hardworking
- Punctuality
- Approachable
- Versatility
- Etiquette
- Problem-solving
- Ability to talk with ease
- Inquisitive
- Even-tempered
- Theory
- Passion
- Intelligence
- Fast learner

- Fun
- Courteous
- Credibility
- Smile
- Pride
- Dedication
- Strong customer service attitudes
- Ability to listen and communicate on a human level
- Capable of providing good and friendly service
- Desire to learn beyond the job description

- Well-groomed
- Respectful
- Quick thinking
- Presence
- Awareness
- Perseverance
- Diligence

When you are able to hire the right person, you save money by not having to re-hire and train another person for the position. Turnover will be less likely and morale will be higher. Just like every other management decision you will make, hiring the right employee requires planning. Some things to keep in mind include:

- Department of Labor regulations on wages and compensation. Be knowledgeable of local, state, and federal laws governing pay rates. Be sure to obtain a copy of the regulations and other information at **www.dol.gov/fairpay**. A copy of the most up-to-date federal labor wages poster should be hung where all employees may view it. Atlantic Publishing Company offers this laminated poster in 11" x 17". You can order it via their Web site (**www.atlantic-pub.com**).

- Federal regulations concerning hiring employees. On the U.S. Department of Labor's Elaws site, **http://www.dol.gov/elaws**, interactive e-tools are provided with easy-to-understand information about a number of the federal employment laws. You should always remain up-to-date with the regulations and watch for any changes that may affect your hiring procedures or your employees.

Now that you know what you are looking for in an employee and you know what to think about in regards to rules and regulations, you need to know where to look to find employees for your restaurant. Here are some ideas:

- **Employment Agencies.** For a fee these agencies will assist you with recruiting a full-time employee. They have a wide range of résumés available to them and have a higher possibility of finding a match for your restaurant and the qualities you are looking for.

- **Temp Agencies.** These give you the option to see and evaluate the employee's performance before taking them on full-time.

- **Job Want Ads.** These types of ads allow you to reach a wide range of potential employees, and ads can be placed in local newspapers, online newspapers, college newspapers, and local magazines.

- **Job Web Sites.** These sites are where many potential employees will go and post their résumés, hoping employers will see them and offer them a job. Some of these sites include:

    o www.jobfactory.com

    o www.hcareers.com

    o www.jobopenings.net/restaurant-jobs/jobs.htm

    o www.starchefsjobfinder.com

    o www.jobsonline.net

    o **hotjobs.yahoo.com/jobs-Restaurant_Food_ Service?refsrc=ysem**

    o **www.monster.com**

    o **www.careerbuilder.com**

- **Your Restaurant's Web Site.** Put an ad on your own business's Web site. A local person may look directly at your site to search for job openings you offer. Many of the major restaurant chains use this method for finding employees.

- **Internal Candidates.** Look at your employees currently on staff to possibly fill an open position. Many of your staff members may want to move up in the restaurant. This could save time and energy because these employees already know and understand the company. These employees should still go through an interview process for the new position.

- **Employee References.** Ask your staff if they have any friends or relatives who may be searching for a job. (If you have a policy against no family members, only ask about friends here.) You may even decide to offer the employee who refers the potential employee a referral bonus. This could be $25 or $50 and is payable once the referred employee has been with the restaurant a certain number of days, such as 30, 60, or 90. This time frame rule will make sure that employees do not try getting friends hired just for the bonus.

- **Customers.** You may find referrals among your customers or may even find a potential employee.

- **Industry Organizations and Web Sites.** These sites may have a place for job postings and résumé searches. An example is:

o National Restaurant Association — **www.restaurant.org**

- **Area Colleges or Universities.** Many school sites will have a job bank for students who are searching for a part-time or full-time job. The restaurant industry is one of the top employers of students.

Be sure to have an employment application on file and available for when a potential employee sees your ad and wishes to fill one out. You will also have potential employees come in at any and all times to fill out an application. Here are two samples taken from *The Restaurant Manager's Handbook,* available from Atlantic Publishing Company (**www.atlantic-pub.com**). The first is an application for a current member of your staff to apply for the open position. The second is a general application for employment. Several other samples can be found in *The Restaurant Manager's Handbook.*

APPLICATION FOR AN IN-HOUSE CANDIDATE

Personal Information (please print)

Name: _____ Date: _____

Address: _____

City: _____ State: _____ Zip: _____

Phone Number: _____

Current Position Information

Current Position: _____

Full Time   Part Time

Length of Employment: _____

Current Supervisor: _____

APPLICATION FOR AN IN-HOUSE CANDIDATE

Position Information: _____

Position Applied For: _____

Department / Group: _____

Full Time   Part Time

Reason(s) for applying for new position (check all that apply):

Opportunity for advancement   Preferred shift

Variety of job duties   Other (please list)

_____

_____

_____

In-House Results to be Filled Out by Supervisor

Accepted   Denied

If accepted, list start date: _____

If denied, check reason:

Did not meet job requirements   Attendence record not acceptable

Another employee with more seniority was selected

Other: _____

Signature of Supervisor: _____

FOOD SERVICE EMPLOYMENT APPLICATION

Notice to Applicant: *We are an Equal Opportunity Employer and do not discriminate on the basis of applicant's race, color, religion, sex, national origin, citizenship, age, physical or mental disability, or any other characteristic.*

Personal Information (please print)

Name: _____

Social Security Number: _____

Address: _____

City: _____ State: _____ Zip: _____

Phone Number: _____

Position Information

Position applied for (check all that apply):

☐ Executive Chef   ☐ Expediter   ☐ Assistant Manager

☐ Host / Hostess   ☐ Baker   ☐ Kitchen Manager

☐ Banquet Manager   ☐ Prep Cook   ☐ Bartender

☐ Beverage Manager   ☐ Pantry Cook   ☐ Server

☐ Bus Person   ☐ Cashier   ☐ Cocktail Server

☐ Counter Person   ☐ Cook   ☐ Dining Room Manager

☐ Other: _____

Have you ever worked for this organization? ☐ Yes   ☐ No

If yes, date(s): _____

FOOD SERVICE EMPLOYMENT APPLICATION

Prior position: _____

Reason(s) for leaving: _____
_____

Education (List from present to past)

School / Institution, Major, Area of Study, Degree, or Number of Years

_____
_____

Other Information
Name of friends and/or relatives employed by this organization:

_____
_____

Position(s) held: _____
_____

If you are eligible, are you interested in health insurance? ☐ Yes ☐ No

Awards / Achievements:

_____
_____
_____
_____

References (Please list at least three people who are not related to you):

Name, Occupation, Phone Number

_____
_____
_____

FOOD SERVICE EMPLOYMENT APPLICATION

Emergency Contact (in the event of an emergency)

Name: _____ Relationship: _____

Address: _____

City: _____ State: _____ Zip: _____

Phone Number: _____

Acknowledgement (please read carefully)

I hereby certify that the information contained in this application form and in my attachments (hereafter made a part of this application) is true and correct to the best of my knowledge and agree to have any of the statements checked by the organization unless I have indicated to the contrary. I authorize the references listed above to provide the company any and all information concerning my previous employment and any pertinent information that they may have. Further, I release all parties and persons from any and all liability for any damages that may result from furnishing such information to the company as well as from the use or disclosure of such information by the organization or any of its agents, employees, or representatives. I understand that any misrepresentation, falsification, or material omission of information on this application may result in my failure to receive an offer or, if I am hired, in my dismissal from employment.

Applicant's Signature: _____

Date: _____

Training Employees

Although waiting tables in other countries is often an honor, in the U.S. it is not considered so. Most of the employees in a restaurant are going to be working mothers, students, retirees, and others looking for part-time work. One way to reduce the turnover so prevalent among restaurants is by investing in training and education for employees.

Most restaurants put new employees directly into their jobs with little or no training. It is the responsibility of the restaurant manager to train and continue to train their employees. Start teaching the employees new areas to work in and show them how the position they hold is important to the overall business organization. Some excellent resources for training employees include:

- *How to Hire, Train, and Keep the Best Employees for your Small Business — With Companion CD-ROM* available from Atlantic Publishing (**www.atlantic-pub.com**).

- *The Waiter & Waitress and WaitStaff Training Handbook: A Complete Guide to the Proper Steps in Service for Food & Beverage Employees* available from Atlantic Publishing (**www.atlantic-pub.com**).

- *The Complete WaitStaff Training Course on VHS and DVD* — A 60-minute waitstaff training video from which your staff will learn how to consistently deliver the quality service that makes customers not only come back, but tell others about their memorable experience. This training tape is ideal as a backbone in your training program for experienced waitstaff who are always looking to learn more or for people who have never waited tables and would like to learn the basics. Certificates are available upon completion. The course is available from Atlantic Publishing (**www.atlantic-pub.com**) and can be purchased in English or Spanish and VHS or DVD format.

One good example of employee training taken to heart is Starbucks. Starbucks is number 16 on Fortune's 100 Best Companies to Work For 2007. (**http://money.cnn.com/magazines/fortune/bestcompanies/2007/ snapshots/16.html**). They were number 29 on the list for 2006. Starbucks is considered one of the best places to work due to their commitment to their employees (which they call their partners). According to the Starbucks Web site, one of their top priorities is to "provide a great work environment and treat each other with respect and dignity" (**http://www.starbucks. com/aboutus/jobcenter_thesbuxexperience.asp**). Every partner or barista (according to **www.wikipedia.com** a barista refers to one who has acquired some level of expertise in the preparation of espresso-based coffee drinks) goes through at least 24 hours of training. Below is a case study on Starbucks employee training taken from Strategic Management: Concepts and Cases, 11th Edition by Arthur A. Thompson and A.J. Strickland III, published by McGraw-Hill.

Starbucks has an excellent training program. They require every barista they hire to go through at least 24 hours of training in the first two to four weeks of their employment. The training in the 24-hour period includes classes on the following:

- History of coffee, preparation of drinks, and retail skills

- 4 hours: coffee knowledge

- 4 hours: Customer Service

- 4-hour workshop called "Brewing the Perfect Cup"

- Cash register skills

- Bean weighing

- Proper bag opening

- Proper capture of the beans so none spill on the floor

- Proper holding of the bag so no air is trapped inside

- Label application on packages so they are 1-inch exactly over the company logo

The preparation training for the beverages takes much of their time as it includes the following:

- Bean grinding

- Milk steaming

- Perfect espresso shot pulling (should be 18 to 23 seconds)

- Recipe memorization

- Preparation practicing

- Specializing beverages to customer specifications

Sessions were also included not only on ordering or preparation of the beverages, but also on cleaning and customer service, including:

- Cleaning the milk from the wand of the espresso machine

- Describing the names of the Italian drinks to customers

- Selling skills for a $875 home espresso machine

- Customer eye contact

- Coffee bin cleanliness

If you are interested in learning more about Starbucks' training program, you can visit their Web site at **www.starbucks.com**.

New employees were also taught and drilled on the Star Skills. Star Skills are three guidelines for interpersonal relationships on the job. These three guidelines are maintaining and enhancing self-esteem, listening and acknowledgement, asking for assistance. New baristas must also memorize rules about the degrees milk must be steamed to, how long shots of espresso can be pulled for, amount of pounds to be given based on what a customer requests (1 pound request should be sure to be 1 pound), how long coffee is allowed to sit in the pot, and what to do with dissatisfied customers.

Management trainees for Starbucks undergo even more intensive training than a new barista. They are required to attend training classes for a minimum of 8 weeks, but as long as 12 weeks. They learn everything the new barista must learn, but also information on operating the sore, the company's practices and procedures as outlined in the operating manual, and management skills.

You may decide to come up with a program on your own that will suit the needs of your restaurant and your staff, you may take one already established, or you might even use one already established and then revise it to better fit your business. Whatever you decide, make sure you choose something. The importance of training can never be stressed enough.

New Employees

Be sure to set up a personnel file for each employee hired. This should include the following information for easy reference:

- Application, which should include current name, address, and phone number

- W-4 form, which includes correct tax information and Social Security Number

- An emergency contact with current phone number

- Employment start date

- Job title given with pay rate (this should be updated with any raises given)

- Any employee evaluations given

- Employee handbook acknowledgement form stating they have read and understand the employee handbook

- A copy of the employee handbook used when the employee was hired

- Any notes on problems, complaints, positive notes, etc.

Be sure each employee is given an employee handbook when they start at your restaurant. A good practice is to have them read through the entire thing during their orientation or their first day on the job. A few great resource tools to help you write your employee handbook if you do not have one already include:

- *Design Your Own Effective Employee Handbook: How to Make the Most of Your Staff with Companion CD-ROM* available from Atlantic Publishing (**www.atlantic-pub.com**).

- *Employee Handbook Creator Guide* available from Atlantic Publishing (**www.atlantic-pub.com**).

Both of these resources will give you samples and walk you through creating your own employee handbook.

Then, be sure each employee signs an acknowledgement form. Here is an example.

EMPLOYEE HANDBOOK ACKNOWLEDGEMENT

My signature below acknowledges I have received a copy of the company's employee handbook and that I understand it is my responsibility to read and understand the information and policies it contains.

I also acknowledge and understand that no part of this handbook constitutes a promise or contract for continued employment. My signature below acknowledges that I understand that my employment with the company is "at will" and that I or my employer can terminate or end the employment relationship at any time and for any reason allowable by law, with or without offering reason and with or without notice or severance compensation of any kind.

I understand that no one can alter the employment relationship through verbal contract and that the only modifications to the employment relationship must be in writing, signed by executive management and the human resources director and myself, and that in absence of any written documentation to the contrary, my employment will continue to be "at will."

I understand and acknowledge that the company has the right, without prior notice, to modify, amend, or terminate policies, practices, benefit plans, and other programs within the limits and requirements imposed by law. The company will make all reasonable efforts to notify employees of any changes to policies or this handbook as soon as possible, via written communication or updates to this handbook.

Employee Signature: _____ Date: _____

Employee Name (print): _____ Title: _____

Evaluating Employees

One of the most important duties when managing employees is evaluating them to see how they are performing. The participants interviewed in this book all used a variety of ways to evaluate their wait staff and kitchen staff. Some of these included:

- Monthly, semi-annual, quarterly, and/or yearly reviews stating specific areas needing improvement

- Meetings

- Observation

- Frequent conversations with employees

- Listening to comments from customers

- Looking at their employee's growth

You can choose to evaluate your employees either formally or informally. Informal evaluations occur on a daily basis and include more of an observation of the employees as they work. In this format, managers are constantly informing employees when they need to improve or when they are doing well. Formal evaluations occur beyond the daily observation of your employees. These types of evaluations can occur on a monthly, quarterly, semi-annually, or yearly basis and include specific measurements of the employee's performance. Either way feedback should be given on ways the employee can improve or positive feedback if the employee is doing well. An annual performance review is a good method for evaluating whether an employee is qualified for promotions or salary increases. This type of review should include the different duties of the employee and a way to measure their performance in each area. A good resource for more information on performance reviews and creating customized performance evaluations is *199 Pre-Written Employee Performance Appraisals: The Complete Guide to Successful Employee Evaluations and Documentation — With Companion CD-ROM* available from Atlantic Publishing (**www.atlantic-pub.com**). For example, here is a sample performance review from that book.

SAMPLE PERFORMANCE APPRAISAL FORM

Employee Name: _____

Job Title: _____

Date of Evaluation: _____

Evaluation Performed By: _____

Scale for Measuring Performance:

5 = Excellent   4 = Good   3 = Average   2 = Below Average   1 = Poor

Attendance:	Score:	Notes:
a. Punctual to work every shift	☐ 5 ☐ 4 ☐ 3 ☐ 2 ☐ 1	
b. Does not call in	☐ 5 ☐ 4 ☐ 3 ☐ 2 ☐ 1	
c. Finishes all tasks before leaving even if shift is over	☐ 5 ☐ 4 ☐ 3 ☐ 2 ☐ 1	
d. Other: _____	☐ 5 ☐ 4 ☐ 3 ☐ 2 ☐ 1	
Areas in this segment that need improvement:		
Comments on this segment:		
Teamwork:	**Score:**	**Notes:**
a. Cooperates with co-workers	☐ 5 ☐ 4 ☐ 3 ☐ 2 ☐ 1	
b. Cooperates with manager	☐ 5 ☐ 4 ☐ 3 ☐ 2 ☐ 1	
c. Helps when short-staffed	☐ 5 ☐ 4 ☐ 3 ☐ 2 ☐ 1	
d. Assists with any area when asked without complaint	☐ 5 ☐ 4 ☐ 3 ☐ 2 ☐ 1	
e. Takes on extra shifts and adapts to schedule changes when needed	☐ 5 ☐ 4 ☐ 3 ☐ 2 ☐ 1	
f. Other		

SAMPLE PERFORMANCE APPRAISAL FORM

Areas in this segment that need improvement:

Comments on this segment:

Initiative:	Score:	Notes:
a. Does tasks without being told	☐ 5 ☐ 4 ☐ 3 ☐ 2 ☐ 1	
b. Asks for assistance when it is needed	☐ 5 ☐ 4 ☐ 3 ☐ 2 ☐ 1	
c. Is a self-starter	☐ 5 ☐ 4 ☐ 3 ☐ 2 ☐ 1	
d. Offers suggestions and improvement ideas	☐ 5 ☐ 4 ☐ 3 ☐ 2 ☐ 1	
e. Other: _____	☐ 5 ☐ 4 ☐ 3 ☐ 2 ☐ 1	

Areas in this segment that need improvement:

Comments on this segment:

Dependability:	Score:	Notes:
a. Does tasks in a timely manner	☐ 5 ☐ 4 ☐ 3 ☐ 2 ☐ 1	
b. Meets deadlines set.	☐ 5 ☐ 4 ☐ 3 ☐ 2 ☐ 1	
c. Has consistent performance	☐ 5 ☐ 4 ☐ 3 ☐ 2 ☐ 1	
d. Other: _____	☐ 5 ☐ 4 ☐ 3 ☐ 2 ☐ 1	

Areas in this segment that need improvement:

Comments on this segment:

Attitude:	Score:	Notes:
a. Freely gives assistance when needed to other employees and management	☐ 5 ☐ 4 ☐ 3 ☐ 2 ☐ 1	
b. Offers a positive contribution to employee morale.	☐ 5 ☐ 4 ☐ 3 ☐ 2 ☐ 1	
c. Takes criticism positively	☐ 5 ☐ 4 ☐ 3 ☐ 2 ☐ 1	
d. Takes pride in work	☐ 5 ☐ 4 ☐ 3 ☐ 2 ☐ 1	
e. Other: _____	☐ 5 ☐ 4 ☐ 3 ☐ 2 ☐ 1	

SAMPLE PERFORMANCE APPRAISAL FORM

Areas in this segment that need improvement:		
Comments on this segment:		

Judgement:	Score:	Notes:
a. Works well under pressure	☐ 5 ☐ 4 ☐ 3 ☐ 2 ☐ 1	
b. Reviews decisions before acting on them	☐ 5 ☐ 4 ☐ 3 ☐ 2 ☐ 1	
c. Other: _____	☐ 5 ☐ 4 ☐ 3 ☐ 2 ☐ 1	

Areas in this segment that need improvement:		
Comments on this segment:		

Specific Job Role:	Score:	Notes:
a. Has knowledge of skills required for position	☐ 5 ☐ 4 ☐ 3 ☐ 2 ☐ 1	
b. Ability to learn new duties or skills as required by position	☐ 5 ☐ 4 ☐ 3 ☐ 2 ☐ 1	
c. Reports to manager or supervisor any issues or problem areas	☐ 5 ☐ 4 ☐ 3 ☐ 2 ☐ 1	
d. Other: _____	☐ 5 ☐ 4 ☐ 3 ☐ 2 ☐ 1	

Areas in this segment that need improvement:		
Comments on this segment:		

Productivity:	Score:	Notes:
a. Is able to complete tasks and duties in a timely manner	☐ 5 ☐ 4 ☐ 3 ☐ 2 ☐ 1	
b. Makes effective use of time while on the clock	☐ 5 ☐ 4 ☐ 3 ☐ 2 ☐ 1	
c. Can handle multiple tasks at once	☐ 5 ☐ 4 ☐ 3 ☐ 2 ☐ 1	
Other: _____	☐ 5 ☐ 4 ☐ 3 ☐ 2 ☐ 1	

Areas in this segment that need improvement:		
Comments on this segment:		

SAMPLE PERFORMANCE APPRAISAL FORM

Safety:	Score:	Notes:
a. Does all tasks safely	☐ 5 ☐ 4 ☐ 3 ☐ 2 ☐ 1	
b. Recognizes safety issues and takes safety of others into consideration	☐ 5 ☐ 4 ☐ 3 ☐ 2 ☐ 1	
c. Other: _____	☐ 5 ☐ 4 ☐ 3 ☐ 2 ☐ 1	
Areas in this segment that need improvement:		
Comments on this segment:		
Customer Service:	**Score:**	**Notes:**
a. Treats all customers with respect and care	☐ 5 ☐ 4 ☐ 3 ☐ 2 ☐ 1	
b. Takes care of customer issues and complaints with no problem	☐ 5 ☐ 4 ☐ 3 ☐ 2 ☐ 1	
c. Other: _____		
Areas in this segment that need improvement:		
Comments on this segment:		

Employee's Excused Absences: _____   Unexcused Absences: _____

Employee has learned the following skills and job duties: _____

_____

Employee is recommended for:

A raise: _____   Amount: $ _____

A promotion: _____

Promoted to: ☐ Manager   ☐ Assistant Manager   ☐ Shift Supervisor

Concluding Comments: _____

_____

Manager's Signature: _____

Manager's Name (printed): _____

Create a Satisfying Environment for Employees

While it is important to attend to the training and support needs of your employees and to be actively involved in recruiting and hiring people who fit your organization, effective managers devote much of their time to motivating their employees to perform over and above the required minimums. While it is important for employees to feel good about what they are doing and feel appreciated, it is still necessary to hold them accountable for results. The best restaurants have productive people who are satisfied with their work environment and who are committed to the company's success. To retain top-notch staff, you will need to create a culture and environment that values your employees and allows and encourages them to reach their potential. Things that provide motivation on the job include:

- Achievement
- Recognition
- Work itself

- Possibility of growth
- Responsibility
- Advancement

Employee Motivation Program

To create a successful motivation program, you must start with the following assumptions:

- Employees start out motivated. A lack of motivation is a learned response fostered by misunderstood or unrealistic expectations.

- Management is responsible for creating a supportive, problem-solving work environment in which necessary resources to perform a task are provided.

- Rewards should encourage high personal performance that is consistent with management objectives.

- Motivation works best when it is based on self-governance.

- Employees need to be treated fairly and consistently.

- Employees deserve timely, honest feedback on their work performance.

The responsibility is on managers to create a motivating environment and continuously monitor the situation to ensure it evolves and stays motivating.

Employee Motivation Rules

Define Expectations. The foundation of a great motivation program is correct goal-setting. Do your employees understand their role in the restaurant? Do they see a connection between their daily duties and the bottom line? Unless the answer is yes to both of those questions, then they are simply showing up and collecting a paycheck.

It is very important for employees to feel ownership and empowerment. Ownership happens when they have goals to achieve that are tied to operational performance. These are called performance goals and the best way to achieve them is to make them SMART.

SMART goals are:

- **Specific:** Well-defined and clear to all parties.

- **Measurable:** You know if the goal is obtainable, how far away completion is, and when it has been achieved.

- **Achievable:** It should be something that is challenging but also within your ability to attain.

- **Realistic:** Within the availability of resources, knowledge, and time.

- **Time-framed:** Set a start and end date and leave enough time to achieve the goal within realistic parameters.

Telling a person to take initiative or do their best is not motivating because these terms mean different things to different people. SMART goals are agreed upon and readily verifiable and quantifiable.

Increase the Value of Work. To make something motivating, it is important to find out what is important to your employees. Most people think that money is the main motivator, but that is actually not the case. Different people are motivated by different things at different times, and the best way to find out what employees value is to ask them directly. Companies have spent thousands of dollars on recognition programs only to find out that the reward is a joke to the staff; instead of getting a company t-shirt, what they really wanted was a company picnic table out back. Here are some examples of things commonly considered valuable:

a) **Flexible Schedules.** Options include employees working more hours on certain days and fewer on others, in fixed or variable schedules. Compressed work weeks offer employees the opportunity to bundle two full weeks of full-time work into a fixed schedule of eight or nine days. In all circumstances, the programs are structured to meet business objectives while recognizing individual needs. Of the managers interviewed, 46 percent said they do offer flex scheduling while 46 percent do not offer flex scheduling. (See the graph in the appendix.)

b) **Job Sharing.** Two or more people splitting position responsibilities is another way to acknowledge personal needs while bringing diversity of experience to a singular position. Individuals sharing jobs and working part-time may reduce benefit costs while retaining talent that may otherwise choose to retire or leave the company. Factors to consider are the need to communicate between position participants and the transferability of knowledge.

c) **Paid Leave Banks.** A structured program that combines vacation, short-term sick leave, personal days, and emergency leave is a way to reward and motivate employees. Although the company retains the right to grant approval for leave, the employee can accrue more discretionary days than with some traditional programs. The costs remain the same for the company, while participants perceive greater control and are more likely to remain content in the long run.

d) **Phased Retirement.** By offering a combination of pension modification and staggered working periods, a program can be structured to reduce overall expenses, motivate and retain the employee, and help meet business objectives.

e) **Developmental Opportunities and Career Planning.** Many individuals express frustration in performing the same responsibilities over and over. The ability of a company to structure career-planning programs, including job rotations, skills training, and project management assignments, are of interest to many employees. Providing opportunities to learn new technologies and methods and accomplish new achievements is significant in capturing prolonged interest from high-potential staff. Giving people the opportunity to gain exposure and implement new programs while building self-esteem and credibility is valuable for both the company and the employee. Opportunity and recognition of accomplishments can prove to be a much more lucrative incentive than any financial considerations a company may offer.

f) **Feedback.** People crave knowing what other people think of their work. Although autonomy is important, so is ready access to and abundant time with managers.

g) **Tangible Rewards.** Small, immediate, concrete, tangible rewards, such as money and gift certificates, are very motivating. The key is to find out what events or activities motivate the employee. Just because you like to watch the game from the corporate box seat does not mean that your accountant feels the same way.

h) **Have Fun.** For well-balanced individuals, their personal lives are more important than their careers. Incentives and benefits that demonstrate an organization's support of a balance are attractive to them.

i) **Pat People on the Back.** Few perks are cheaper, easier, or more effective than recognition. Recognition can take a variety of forms. The basic premise is to catch people doing something right and then tell them and others about it.

j) **Share the Perks of Your Business.** Is there an aspect of your business that you could turn into an inexpensive employee benefit? Maybe you get merchandise or certificates from suppliers. Instead of keeping those for the managers, share them with your top performers. Let employees share in perks you provide to your clients.

k) **Feed Employees.** Provide monthly in-house luncheons, order pizza on a Friday afternoon, or bake a cake for each employee's birthday. These are fun events that encourage intermingling and foster loyalty.

l) **Offer Advancement Opportunities.** One of the best incentives for ambitious people is opportunity. Fill management positions by promoting from within, ensuring that long-term employees have a chance to rise and that new employees have an incentive to stay.

Provide Support. For people to be motivated, you must set the groundwork by offering a supportive work environment. No amount of goal-setting or original rewards will work if your employees do not feel they are given the resources and materials necessary for success. You must ask yourself, "Do my employees feel it is possible to achieve this goal?" Support means providing resources, training, and encouragement; essentially, managers need to pave the way for success.

Take this concept beyond lip-service and commit to supporting your employees. Support comes back to the notion of validation; if an employee does not feel he or she has been given the tools necessary to succeed, she will feel invalidated and unworthy. Nothing is less motivating than the feeling of helplessness and being sent out to sink or swim. From your first day of orientation to the employee's last day on the job, you must provide all the information, background, training, and encouragement necessary to be successful. Employees need to feel that management is working hard to help them achieve their performance goals.

No-Cost Ways to Recognize Employees

Provide Information. Information is power and employees want to be empowered with the information they need to know to do their jobs more effectively. And employees want to know how they are doing and how the company is doing in its business. Open the channels of communication in your organization to allow employees to be informed, ask questions, and share information.

Encourage Involvement. Managers today are faced with an incredible number of opportunities and problems and, as the speed of business continues to increase dramatically, the amount of time that they have to make decisions continues to decrease. Involving employees in decision-making, especially when the decisions affect them directly, is respectful and practical. Those closest to the problem typically have the best insight as to what to do. As you involve others, you increase their commitment and ease in implementing new ideas or change.

Foster Independence. Few employees want their every action to be closely monitored. Most employees appreciate having the flexibility to do their jobs as they see fit. Giving people latitude increases the chance that they will perform as you desire — and bring additional initiative, ideas, and energy to their jobs.

Increase Visibility. Everyone appreciates getting credit when it is due. Occasions to share the successes of employees with others are almost limitless. Giving employees new opportunities to perform, learn, and grow as a form of recognition and thanks is highly motivating for most people.

Reward Success

Like feedback, rewards for success must be given in a timely manner. Rewards, even highly valuable ones, lose their motivating potential unless they are given at the correct time. It is the timing of reinforcements that lets employees know which behaviors are being encouraged. While it seems quite obvious, it is often not done — after going through all the administration required, their reward is sometimes not actually given for weeks after the fact. Delay between performance and feedback dilutes the effectiveness of the reward, so it is imperative that you be prepared with your system of motivation and plan ahead for the administrative aspects.

Reward success consistently and fairly. There is nothing more de-motivating than a reward that is given under unfair circumstances or out of preferential treatment. Establish the parameters of your reward system and treat all employees with the same rules.

Maintaining Good Employee Relations

Management attitudes create the culture of an organization. The following tips can be applied to create a culture that is satisfying to employees and productive for the organization.

Be Available for Discussions. Let employees know that they can go to management with problems and concerns. Ensure that management conduct creates an environment of trust and confidence. Managers must take concerns seriously and address them promptly. Do not put people off; they will not forget it.

Maintain Confidentiality. When employees discuss matters of concern to management, their confidences must be respected. When confidences must be shared to resolve the problem, the employee should be told.

Give Uninterrupted Attention to Employees. Do not allow visitors and phone calls when discussing an important matter with employees. Let your actions convey that the employee is important to you. Give employees the focused attention they deserve.

Conduct Well-Organized Meetings. Meetings should provide valuable information and solicit employee feedback. Avoid surprises in the agenda.

Do Not Criticize Employees In Public. If an employee must be corrected, do so privately. Never point out an employee's mistakes to or in front of other employees. When corrective action is necessary, be timely, clear, and accurate. Provide the employee with concrete examples to ensure that he or she understands the problem so he or she can improve the performance.

Treat All Employees the Same. Perceptions of special treatment are damaging to morale and create potential legal liability.

Remember the Small Things. Consider celebrating birthdays, company anniversaries, and special events and give recognition when due. Even if you only give out a birthday card and a little bag of candy for each employee's birthday, it still shows you care and are attentive to your employees.

Encourage Employee Input. Share problems and challenges when appropriate and ask for suggestions on how to deal with them.

Delegate and Develop. Delegate new, challenging tasks to employees; provide opportunities for employees to develop new skills.

Welcome Change. Welcome change as a means for you, your employees, and the company to progress to a better future. Generate enthusiasm for change.

Support Organizational Goals. Work as a team, ensuring there are no interdepartmental battlegrounds that are counterproductive.

Be Human. Enjoy your work and employees. Share your enthusiasm. Make yourself approachable and willing to listen.

Chapter Conclusion

As you have seen from reading the studies provided by the restaurant managers and owners presented in this book employees are vital to the success of a restaurant. Managers should take great care when hiring, training, and evaluating employees. Your customers are going to be waited on and almost constantly see the employees you have in your establishment. That means these employees should be well-trained, polite, and respectful of your customers. If they are not, you may lose your customers. A restaurant cannot survive without them, so the way you deal with your employees should be a top priority.

Chapter 2

The Restaurant

When interviewing these managers, it was not just employees I asked about. Besides the employees, you also need many things to actually run a restaurant. These include equipment, food, safety rules, and marketing and advertising for the restaurant. This chapter will touch on all these aspects of the restaurant and provide you with some helpful tools for each area.

Equipment

A restaurant cannot run without its equipment, although many of the managers have said they have made do without all the equipment they needed to get started. Whether you purchase new, used, or decide to make do or go without certain equipment for the restaurant, always make sure employees are trained on how to use each piece of equipment. Accidents can occur when proper training is not given.

Here is a list of furniture, fixtures, and equipment that you may or may not have or use depending on the type of restaurant you have. This is not a complete list, but just a sampling of what may or may not be used.

- Bar
- Ice machine
- High chairs

- Heat lamps
- Bar stools
- Ladles

- Baking trays
- Chairs
- Fryer(s)
- Dolly
- Food cutter
- Broiler
- Blender
- Dishes
- Dishwasher
- Coffee maker
- Napkins
- Meat grinder
- Roll warmer
- Refrigerator
- Potholders
- Convection oven
- Spoons
- Cheese melter
- Portion scales
- Toaster
- Soap dispensers

- Benches
- Pans
- Coat rack
- Mixer
- Cash register
- Coat rack
- Linens
- Freezer(s)
- Microwave
- Cheese grater
- Garbage disposal
- Pots
- Signage
- Can opener(s)
- Slicer
- Spatulas
- Sandwich table
- Soda system
- Room dividers
- Security system
- Tongs

- Preparation sinks
- Utensil rack
- Steam kettle
- Baker's bins and tables
- Pressureless steamer
- Washer and Dryer
- Storage shelves
- Prep and steam tables
- Utensils
- Ventilation system
- Beverage-dispensing system
- Three-compartment sink

This equipment can be purchased through local retailers, restaurants going out of business or ones that are upgrading to new equipment, eBay, the Internet, and other places. Some great resources for finding restaurant equipment suppliers are:

- dmoz Open Directory: **http://dmoz.org/Business/Hospitality/ Food_Service/Tools_and_Equipment**

- Business.com: **http://www.business.com/directory/food_and_ beverage/restaurants_and_foodservice/equipment_and_supplies**

- Frasers: **http://www.frasers.com/directory/companies.cfm?Office ID=0&UserSearch=&SearchBy=A&Keyword=&ProductID=20 313&WFrom=B&ParentID=3&GPID=0&Taxonomy=5**

- PowerSourcing: **http://www.powersourcing.com/se/restaurant equipment.htm**

- Restaurant Solutions Inc.: **http://www.restaurantsolutionsinc. com/resources.htm**

- Google Directory: **http://www.google.com/Top/Business/ Hospitality/Food_Service/Tools_and_Equipment**

You can also check out the National Restaurant Association's Web site, where you can search vendors and retailers by subject or type of merchandise you are looking for. See the equipment specific search at **http://www.restaurant. org/business/buyersguide/categories.cfm?SuperCat=E**.

Computers

All the participants I interviewed use computers to keep their daily records. According to an article I recently read, the rise of computer usage among restaurants is up. Restaurants use computers to keep track of daily records, to keep track of inventory, create menu ordering and billing, employee payroll, and to create employee schedules. Some restaurants also create and maintain a restaurant Web site.

For recordkeeping and accounting, I recommend using one of these two programs. If you make use of a point-of-sale system these may not be useful for you.

- QuickBooks: **www.quickbooks.com**

- Peachtree: **www.peachtree.com**

For inventory tracking, I recommend the following software:

- iPro: **http://www.foodsoftware.com/Product_0004_01.asp**

- AccuBar (for liquor inventory and tracking): **http://www.accubar. com**

For scheduling employees, try the following software:

- Employee Schedule Software: **http://www.espsoftware.com/**

There are many software programs you can purchase for use with your restaurant's computer to do many tasks for the manager. Scheduling, inventory, and ordering are simplified with these easy-to-use programs and can free up some of your time as a manager to be able to do other important duties around the restaurant.

When it comes to choosing a computer, there are a few basics you should look for:

Hard Drive Space: Your computer should come with a minimum of 40 GB of memory. Most computers sold nowadays are sold with a minimum of 60 GB. The more programs you plan on installing, the more memory you will need. It may be better to go for more than not enough.

System Memory: Your computer should be no less than 512 MB RAM. A lot of computers nowadays come with 1024 MB. The more system memory you have the better if you plan to run multiple programs at once.

Other things you should look for, depending on what you plan to do on the computer, include: brand, processor, programs, drives (CD, DVD), and graphics card.

Once you have your computer, I recommend downloading a free anti-virus program. Most computers will come with a free trial of a major brand name of software, but these free trials will expire. I suggest just going right ahead and installing the free one so you do not forget. AVG is a good program that I use on my own computer. The free edition is available at **http://free. grisoft.com/doc/2/.**

Food is one of those most important parts of a restaurant. The managers in this book have shared the types of food they serve, where they purchase their food, and whether they prefer fresh or frozen foods. Of the participants interviewed, none of them use only frozen foods, 58 percent use a mix of fresh and frozen foods, and 42 percent use only fresh foods (see chart in the appendix). Many of the participants purchase the foods from local vendors.

The National Restaurant Association offers a buyer's guide for restaurants to search for products — one being food. The food subcategories include seafood, soups, cheese, fish, bread, and frozen and fresh meats. You can do a full search of the vendors listed at **http://www.restaurant.org/business/ buyersguide/categories.cfm?SuperCat=F**. You should be able to find local food vendors through your local chamber of commerce or by searching the Web for local food vendors.

Alcohol

Offering alcohol in your restaurant can set it apart from the others in the area that do not. Most people enjoy a glass of wine or beer with their dinner and providing that enjoyment will make your establishment stand out. Of the managers interviewed in this book, an amazing 96 percent said they serve alcohol in their restaurants, while the other 4 percent said they do not yet serve alcohol but plan to in the future. State agencies that regulate alcohol control can be found through the National Restaurant Association at **http://www.restaurant.org/government/state/agencies_all.cfm**. A list of each state is provided with a link to that state's alcohol regulation agency. Restaurants are required to be licensed to sell alcohol, and you can find many resources from your state agency when deciding whether or not to serve alcohol.

To keep your restaurant protected be sure to train your servers to faithfully check the identification cards of anyone requesting alcohol that does not appear over the age of 40. It is always better to be safe than sorry. Customers may get annoyed, but let your servers know that, if those customers want alcohol to remain in the restaurant, this policy needs to be enforced. If alcohol is served to someone underage the restaurant could lose its liquor license and possibly face even harsher punishments.

To find alcohol vendors, I recommend making use of the list the National Restaurant Association provides at **http://www.restaurant.org/business/ buyersguide/categories.cfm?SuperCat=Z**.

A few resources on serving alcohol in your restaurant include:

- *The Responsible Serving of Alcoholic Beverages: A Complete Staff Training Course for Bars, Restaurants, and Caterers With Companion CD-ROM* by Beth Dugan, available from Atlantic Publishing Company (**www. atlantic-pub.com**, 978-0-910627-63-4).

- Alcohol Service Poster Series from Atlantic Publishing. These contain essential information, drink photos, recipes, and more, and they help increase sales and grab attention. Posters are laminated to reduce wear and tear and measure 11" x 17". You can purchase the entire set or each poster individually.

  o Series of 7 Posters Item #ASP-PS

  o 12 Classic Cocktails with Recipes #CC-PS

  o 12 Popular Cocktails with Recipes #PC-PS

  o Types of Beer #TOB-PS

  o Categories of Liquor #COL-PS

  o 10 Types of Martinis #TOM-PS

  o Drink Garnishes #DG-PS

   ° Common Box Abbreviations #GBA-PS

- Alcohol Awareness Posters: Alcohol awareness is an important issue. This poster series covers ten fundamental topics and should be posted in any establishment that serves alcohol. Posters are laminated to reduce wear and tear and measure 11" x 17". You can purchase the whole set or only the posters you need.

   ° Series of 10 Posters Item #AAP-PS

   ° Right to Refuse #RTR-PS

   ° One Drink Equals #ODE-PS

   ° Spotting a Fake ID #FID-PS

   ° Symptoms of Intoxication #SIO-PS

   ° We Check IDs #CID-PS

   ° Drinking & Pregnancy #D&P-PS

   ° Blood Alcohol Content Chart - Female #BACF-PS

   ° Blood Alcohol Content Chart - Male #BACM-PS

   ° Don't Drink & Drive #DDD-PS

   ° Alcohol Slows Reaction Times #ASR-PS

Also see the Appendix, where I have provided a resource list for restaurant managers.

Advertising and Marketing

Advertising and marketing are an important part of your restaurant's success. Advertise locally with banners, billboards, ads in local papers, sponsor a little league team, join the chamber of commerce, provide coupons in local coupons magazines, and have a Web site. Other ways to draw attention to your restaurant include adding activities to the restaurant, providing discounts for returning customers, etc. Below we go into more detail on each of these areas.

Banners: You can place banners at local events, such as fundraisers, school events, car shows, holiday get-togethers, and other such events. In Ocala, Florida, many businesses participate in the March of Dimes, an awareness and fundraising walk for premature babies. Businesses can provide banners to display along the walk for a fee, but with so many walkers, it is definitely worth the fee charged to include your business banner along the walk route. During the walk, booths are provided by local businesses as a rest stop of sorts where they provide the tired walkers with drinks, snacks, and business trinkets (pens, water bottles, etc.). You could try that as well. It is for a good cause and also gets information out about your business.

Billboards: If you have the advertising budget, a billboard may be a good option. Most cities have a highway or interstate somewhere close by where advertising may be valuable for restaurants wanting the weary drivers to stop and eat at their establishment. There may also be billboards throughout the city or town in which your restaurant is located — maybe near a busy street or local hangout place, such as a park or town square.

Ads: Purchasing advertising space in a local newspaper, magazine, etc. could be a good option for your restaurant. Local newspapers and magazines will more than likely also have Web sites where you could also get your ad placed. Another option to get your ad placed could be the local theatre's program.

For each production they may be looking for advertisers to include. There are always a few minutes before the play where people are waiting and will look through the entire program. You could even include an ad that allows theatre goers to bring the program in for a discount of some sort after the play. This is a way to get the restaurant noticed and even bring customers in time after time.

Radio: Purchase radio air time and provide a catchy ad for your restaurant. Make is something the listener will remember, but not something they will get annoyed with. A great idea to get your name out there is to offer the hosts of the shows coupons for Dinner for Two meals or something they can offer as prizes for their radio contests. The station I listen to every morning has one contest in which they provide a local restaurant's coupon. I still have not won it, but I have heard that restaurant's name often and even visited myself.

Sponsorship: Sponsoring a Little League team or city athletic team may be a good way to get your name noticed as well. Generally the advertiser only needs to purchase the team uniform (shirts and/or caps), which will include your restaurant's name, the members will wear during each game. This is an excellent tool as you are not only helping out kids, but are also getting your business's name out to all the family and friends who attend the games. Many times sponsorship may also include putting a sign on the fence of the field with your business information on it.

Join the chamber of commerce or other local business clubs: Joining the chamber of commerce in the city/county in which your restaurant is located is a great idea. You will be adding yourself to the community of businesses in your area. For example, the chamber of commerce in my local community offers many great benefits to those who join. According to **http://www.ocalacc.com/ocala_florida/templates/standard.aspx?arti cleid=2&zoneid=4**, these benefits include:

- Visibility (They include your business listing in their white and yellow page listings and online listing.)

- Increased business

- Recognition, credibility, and influence

- Savings and discounts

- Awareness through regular communications

- Development and growth through training and education

- Expansion through exclusive networking and involvement opportunities

- Efficiency through convenient access to professional services and resources

The benefits the chamber membership offers could be just what your restaurant needs to succeed. There are also other local business clubs you can join, and I recommend looking into each one your city or town offers.

Provide coupons in local coupon magazines. The last two places I have lived have both had local *Mint Magazines.* These magazines include coupons for restaurants and other service industry places. They are delivered once a month, and I look forward to them. I have chosen to eat at many of those establishments simply because of the coupon offered. I did not even know about some of the places until I received my magazine in the mail. There may or may not be a *Mint Magazine* or something similar in your city or town. But, if there is, it is definitely worth looking into. Visit **http://www. mintmagazine.com/about.asp?loc=1** for more information about the *Mint Magazine.*

Other coupon offerings. You may also decide to offer coupons in other types of publications, create your own flyer or brochure to mail out, or a coupon to give out with your customer receipts. Doing this may prompt customers to return again to use the valuable coupon. If you decide to create a flyer or brochure or something along those lines to mail out, I recommend the following sites which offer great printing costs:

- Vista Print: **www.vistaprint.com**

- Overnight Prints: **www.overnightprints.com**

- Online Print House: **www.onlineprinthouse.com**

You might also try purchasing a high quality inkjet printer instead if you have a smaller budget. I prefer the sites listed above because they offer great products for very low cost. With Vista Print you can join their e-mail list. I did this, and I receive e-mails a few times a week offering free items (such as 100 free standard postcards or 20 free magnets).

When I asked the participants if they offer coupons in advertising, I got mixed results: 13 percent said they sometimes offer coupons in advertising, 48 percent said they offer no coupons in advertising, and 39 percent said they do offer coupons in advertising. The type of establishment you have may determine whether or not you will provide coupons.

A Web site. A Web site can be a great tool for your restaurant. With your Web site you can include your menu, your hours, accept reservations, have contests, tell about special events coming up, offer printable coupons, offer a newsletter, and provide photos and testimonials from real customers. More information on each of these opportunities is below.

- **Menu**. Including your menu will allow potential customers to go ahead and search what your restaurant has to offer. Someone who is unsure if your establishment is where they want to go may make a decision by seeing your menu and discovering that you are serving exactly what they are looking for. I recommend including photos of some or all of your dishes so their eyes may decide what they want to eat.

- **Hours.** Include the hours you are open and what days. If a potential customer is trying to make sure you are still open, they can find it easily and quickly right on your site.

- **Reservations.** Accepting reservations online is an excellent opportunity to reach hi-tech customers who are Internet savvy. I myself like to make reservations online and find it fast, easy, and simple. It also prevents customers from being frustrated when the employee taking reservations on the phone is busy.

- **Contests.** You can provide contests on your Web site. You can advertise these in your restaurant, on your menu, or through an ad placed in a local paper or magazine to help draw people to your site. You can offer a contest that gives the winner a free meal, free dessert, a free t-shirt, or something else along those lines. You might even provide Dinner for Two coupons.

- **Special Events.** Tell about the special events coming up at your restaurant. You can even have people RSVP right there online. Or you can lead people to your site from other forms of advertising so they can find all the details about the event.

- **Printable Coupons.** You can provide printable coupons for those who find your site and decide to visit. It may only be for 10 percent off or a free drink, but many people will find that is enough of an incentive to drive them right to you.

- **Newsletter.** Make a newsletter or weekly journal available on your Web site. You can ask your staff to provide a note, thought of the week, or just a message of how the week was. This can be included in your newsletter or journal.

- **Photos and Testimonials.** Take photos often at the restaurant — especially when you have event nights or special activities going on. Make sure you let the customers know to check your site and see themselves. It could make them feel like mini-celebrities and will hopefully drive visitors to your site. This could make that first-time guest a repeat customer. Also provide testimonials from customers. You can give guests comment cards and request they fill them out and give permission for you to use their testimonials on the site. Potential customers may be more likely to visit your restaurant if they can see that real people actually cared enough about what they ate, saw, and how they were treated that they will want to visit as well. You could also put a photo up of the customer who provided the testimonial just to make it all the more real for the potential customers.

- **Provide Employee Space.** A good option for getting your staff organized and always in touch is by providing a log in area that only they can get into. Here you can post the schedule, day off request forms, meeting dates, and other important information your employees need to know. You can even include a chat area where they can log in and visit with other members of the staff. Or, even better, just a message board where employees can leave messages, questions, comments, or put messages up about vacations or time off.

There are so many things you can do with your Web site. A very cheap place to get a Web site where you can choose a .com, .net, or other site type is **GoDaddy.com**. I have my own Web site through them and pay only a small fee a year for the use of my site.

Entertainment

Adding activities to your restaurant can provide your establishment with something that others lack and allow it to be set apart from the other businesses in your area. Many of the restaurants in this book provide different forms of entertainment for their customers. This can be a major bonus for your establishment, as it can give it an edge and draw in different crowds. Some forms of entertainment you can provide include:

- **Televisions.** Providing at least one television or multiple ones can be a plus. You can have the weather channel or news channel on. You might consider the size of the television if you decide to have fight nights, as you will want larger televisions for those events.

- **Game Area.** If you want to be more family oriented, try including a game area with video games and even a pool table or two.

- **Karaoke.** Karaoke can be fun to include on your calendar once or twice a month.

- **Live Bands or a DJ.** Have local bands come play at your restaurant maybe once a month or just on special occasions. You may be able to pull in a large crowd if you advertise it correctly. Having a DJ every so often can also be a plus — maybe even provide a small dance floor.

- **Comedy Night.** Local comics doing stand-up can be a fun and different way to entertain your customers.

- **Movie Night.** This can be a fun family event. You could even give out free popcorn to customers who come. You may consider doing this event in a private room or banquet hall to avoid bothering other customers.

- **Kids Night.** You could hire a magician or clown and make it a family night out. Maybe try this once a month or once every quarter. You can also provide a special kids dinner.

- **Fight Night.** Turning all the televisions in the establishment to a specific fight can be a popular way to pull in a crowd. You may have to have HBO or PPV options on your cable plan in order to purchase these programs.

These are just a few ideas and not all of them may not work for your restaurant. Try different things until you find what works best for your business. Once you find a few things that work you can begin to do a regular schedule of these things. Make sure you add them to your Web site.

Safety and Risk Management

Safety should be a major concern for you as a restaurant manager. This should extend to your employees and customers as well.

Kitchen and Food Safety

Ensuring your patrons and staff are not injured on the premises is more than a matter of caring for their well-being — it is an essential part of avoiding a business-threatening lawsuit and lengthy downtime. Labor savings, insurance savings, workers' compensation reductions, and sick pay savings — not to mention staying out of civil court — all come from putting safety procedures in place — and sticking to them.

Here are some ways to do this:

- **Keep equipment in working order.** Make sure that equipment, tools, machinery, and substances are in safe condition.

- **Talk to your workers about safety in the workplace.** Encourage open discussion.

- **Hygiene.** Maintain safe and hygienic facilities, including toilets, eating areas, and first aid.

- **Staff training.** Offer information, training, and supervision for all workers.

- **Involve your staff.** Implement processes to inform workers and involve them in decisions that may affect their health and safety at work.

- **Safety procedures.** Implement processes for identifying hazards and assessing and controlling risks.

- **Accident book.** Record work-related injuries and illnesses.

- **Be observant.** Pay attention to safe work. Your business will not only become more competitive, but you can help stop the pain and suffering from workplace injury or fatality.

- **Post safety signs.** Ensure safety signs, usually available for free from your local Department of Health or Labor or your appliance manufacturers, are posted around your kitchen. These will include details on how to safely lift heavy items, directions on proper signage for slippery floors, and dangerous equipment, as well as rules on who handles jobs like lighting gas pilots, changing light bulbs, and sharpening knives. Atlantic Publishing offers a 10-poster set of workplace safety posters in both English and Spanish. Communicate important information to your employees by posting these colorful, four-color informative safety and human resource posters throughout your workplace. To order this set visit **www.atlantic-pub.com** or call 800-814-1132 (Item # WPP-PS, $79.95).

First Aid and Safety

A restaurant with poorly trained employees can lead to hazardous conditions, another good reason to thoroughly train your employees. They need to be trained on how to handle first-aid safety emergencies.

Have a safety plan in place and train your employees to implement the elements of this plan. Train them so they can respond in a calm and quick manner. Safety training materials can be found on The Training Network's Web site at **www.safetytrainingnetwork.com**.

Accidents and Safety

Any person or business can have an accident, but you can reduce your risk. Here are a few ways to do so:

- Ground your electrical outlets.
- Clean walkways and clear clutter.
- Shovel and salt walks and steps in the winter.
- Provide adequate outdoor lighting.
- Place rails along steps.
- Provide adequate interior lighting.
- Install solid doors.
- Put good locks on windows and doors.
- Have a quality security system installed.

These are only some of the possibilities. Assign someone to be your safety coordinator who can plan and train employees about your evacuation plans, arrange training with local organizations, and be on the lookout for safety problems and concerns.

Kitchen Safety

The restaurant business has many potential safety hazards. Knives, hot ovens, fryers, slicers, grinders, glass, and wet or greasy floors are only some of the hazards your staff faces every day. Many accidents can be prevented with good training. An excellent source for more information on safety for your restaurant is available from Atlantic Publishing Company. *HACCP & Sanitation in Restaurants and Food Service Operations: A Practical Guide Based on the USDA Food Code — With Companion CD-ROM* (**www.atlantic-pub.com**, 800-814-1132, 978-0-910627-35-1) is a great wealth of information and includes a CD with all the forms and checklists in the book available for easy use.

222222222222222222222

Chapter 3

Management Skills

The managers profiled throughout the pages of this book believe there are many things it takes to be a good manager. These things, as well as the qualities they believe they possess that help them, include:

- Ability to adapt
- Ability to be firm but fair
- Ability to multitask
- Ability to simplify
- Ability to stay focused
- Ability to do all jobs required
- Being hands-on
- Being humble
- Caring
- Communication skills
- Courage
- Desire to know employees

- Ability to delegate
- Ability to handle stress
- Ability to relate
- Accountability
- Adaptability
- Backbone
- Calmness
- Camaraderie
- Commitment
- Consistency
- Creativity
- Experience in motivating people

- Diplomacy
- Education
- Empowerment
- Firmness
- Experience
- Good eye for detail
- Honesty
- Helping employees see their value
- Humility
- Independence
- Leadership
- Knowledge of how to build teams
- Motivator
- Open-mindedness
- Outgoing
- Organizational skills
- Passion
- Patience
- People friendly
- People person
- Perceptiveness
- Professional
- Respect
- Quick decision making skills
- Responsible
- Sense of humor
- Straightforwardness
- Training
- Verbal skills
- Versatility
- Willingness to teach
- Work well with others

What qualities do you possess? What qualities do you need to work on to make your management performance better?

This information is provided from the U.S. Department of Labor, Bureau of Labor Statistics at **http://www.bls.gov/oco/ocos024.htm**. It is information about restaurant management and training, qualifications, and advancement for food service managers.

NATURE OF WORK

Food service managers are responsible for the daily operations of restaurants and other establishments that prepare and serve meals and beverages to customers. Besides coordinating activities among various departments, such as kitchen, dining room, and banquet operations, food service managers ensure that customers are satisfied with their dining experience. In addition, they oversee the inventory and ordering of food, equipment, and supplies and arrange for the routine maintenance and upkeep of the restaurant, its equipment, and facilities. Managers generally are responsible for all of the administrative and human-resource functions of running the business, including recruiting new employees and monitoring employee performance and training.

In most full-service restaurants and institutional food service facilities, the management team consists of a general manager, one or more assistant managers, and an executive chef. The executive chef is responsible for all food preparation activities, including running kitchen operations, planning menus, and maintaining quality standards for food service. In limited-service eating places, such as sandwich shops, coffee bars, or fast-food establishments, managers, not executive chefs, are responsible for supervising routine food preparation operations. Assistant managers in full-service facilities generally oversee service in the dining rooms and banquet areas. In larger restaurants and fast-food or other food service facilities that serve meals daily and maintain longer hours, individual assistant managers may supervise different shifts of workers. In smaller restaurants, formal titles may be less important, and one person may undertake the work of one or more food service positions. For example, the executive chef also may be the general manager or even sometimes an owner. (For additional information on these other workers, see material on top executives and chefs, cooks, and food preparation workers elsewhere in the Handbook.)

NATURE OF WORK

One of the most important tasks of food service managers is assisting executive chefs as they select successful menu items. This task varies by establishment depending on the seasonality of menu items, the frequency with which restaurants change their menus, and the introduction of daily or weekly specials. Many restaurants rarely change their menus while others make frequent alterations. Managers or executive chefs select menu items, taking into account the likely number of customers and the past popularity of dishes. Other issues considered when planning a menu include whether there was any unserved food left over from prior meals that should not be wasted, the need for variety, and the seasonal availability of foods. Managers or executive chefs analyze the recipes of the dishes to determine food, labor, and overhead costs and to assign prices to various dishes. Menus must be developed far enough in advance that supplies can be ordered and received in time.

Managers or executive chefs estimate food needs, place orders with distributors, and schedule the delivery of fresh food and supplies. They plan for routine services or deliveries, such as linen services or the heavy cleaning of dining rooms or kitchen equipment, to occur during slow times or when the dining room is closed. Managers also arrange for equipment maintenance and repairs, and coordinate a variety of services such as waste removal and pest control. Managers or executive chefs receive deliveries and check the contents against order records. They inspect the quality of fresh meats, poultry, fish, fruits, vegetables, and baked goods to ensure that expectations are met. They meet with representatives from restaurant supply companies and place orders to replenish stocks of tableware, linens, paper products, cleaning supplies, cooking utensils, and furniture and fixtures.

NATURE OF WORK

Managers must be good communicators. They need to speak well, often in several languages, with a diverse clientele and staff. They must motivate employees to work as a team, to ensure that food and service meet appropriate standards. Managers also must ensure that written supply orders are clear and unambiguous.

Managers interview, hire, train, and, when necessary, fire employees. Retaining good employees is a major challenge facing food service managers. Managers recruit employees at career fairs, contact schools that offer academic programs in hospitality or culinary arts, and arrange for newspaper advertising to attract additional applicants. Managers oversee the training of new employees and explain the establishment's policies and practices. They schedule work hours, making sure that enough workers are present to cover each shift. If employees are unable to work, managers may have to call in alternates to cover for them or fill in themselves when needed. Some managers may help with cooking, clearing tables, or other tasks when the restaurant becomes extremely busy.

Food service managers ensure that diners are served properly and in a timely manner. They investigate and resolve customers' complaints about food quality or service. They monitor orders in the kitchen to determine where backups may occur, and they work with the chef to remedy any delays in service. Managers direct the cleaning of the dining areas and the washing of tableware, kitchen utensils, and equipment to comply with company and government sanitation standards. Managers also monitor the actions of their employees and patrons on a continual basis to ensure the personal safety of everyone. They make sure that health and safety standards and local liquor regulations are obeyed.

NATURE OF WORK

In addition to their regular duties, food service managers perform a variety of administrative assignments, such as keeping employee work records, preparing the payroll, and completing paperwork to comply with licensing laws and reporting requirements of tax, wage and hour, unemployment compensation, and Social Security laws. Some of this work may be delegated to an assistant manager or bookkeeper, or it may be contracted out, but most general managers retain responsibility for the accuracy of business records. Managers also maintain records of supply and equipment purchases and ensure that accounts with suppliers are paid.

Technology influences the jobs of food service managers in many ways, enhancing efficiency and productivity. Many restaurants use computers to track orders, inventory, and the seating of patrons. Point-of-service (POS) systems allow servers to key in a customer's order, either at the table, using a hand-held device, or from a computer terminal in the dining room, and send the order to the kitchen instantaneously so preparation can begin. The same system totals and prints checks, functions as a cash register, connects to credit card authorizers, and tracks sales. To minimize food costs and spoilage, many managers use inventory-tracking software to compare the record of sales from the POS with a record of the current inventory. Some establishments enter an inventory of standard ingredients and suppliers into their POS system. When supplies of particular ingredients run low, they can be ordered directly from the supplier using preprogrammed information. Computers also allow restaurant and food service managers to keep track of employee schedules and paychecks more efficiently.

Food service managers use the Internet to track industry news, find recipes, conduct market research, purchase supplies or equipment, recruit employees, and train staff. Internet access also makes service to customers more efficient. Many restaurants maintain Web sites

NATURE OF WORK

that include menus and online promotions, provide information about the restaurant's location, and offer patrons the option to make a reservation.

Managers tally the cash and charge receipts received and balance them against the record of sales. They are responsible for depositing the day's receipts at the bank or securing them in a safe place. Finally, managers are responsible for locking up the establishment, checking that ovens, grills, and lights are off, and switching on alarm systems.

Working Conditions

Food service managers are among the first to arrive in the morning and the last to leave at night. Long hours — 12 to 15 per day, 50 or more per week, and sometimes 7 days a week — are common. Managers of institutional food service facilities, such as school, factory, or office cafeterias, work more regular hours because the operating hours of these establishments usually conform to the operating hours of the business or facility they serve. However, hours for many managers are unpredictable.

Managers should be calm, flexible, and able to work through emergencies, such as a fire or flood, in order to ensure everyone's safety. Managers also should be able to fill in for absent workers on short notice. Managers often experience the pressures of simultaneously coordinating a wide range of activities. When problems occur, it is the manager's responsibility to resolve them with minimal disruption to customers. The job can be hectic, and dealing with irate customers or uncooperative employees can be stressful.

Managers also may experience the typical minor injuries of other restaurant workers, such as muscle aches, cuts, or burns. They might endure physical discomfort from moving tables or chairs to accommodate large parties, receiving and storing daily supplies from vendors, or making minor repairs to furniture or equipment.

NATURE OF WORK

Training, Other Qualifications, and Advancement

Experience in the food services industry, whether as a full-time waiter or waitress or as a part-time or seasonal counter attendant, is essential training for a food services manager. Many food service management companies and national or regional restaurant chains recruit management trainees from 2- and 4-year college hospitality management programs which require internships and real-life experience to graduate. Some restaurant chains prefer to hire people with degrees in restaurant and institutional food service management, but they often hire graduates with degrees in other fields who have demonstrated experience, interest, and aptitude. Many restaurant and food service manager positions — particularly self-service and fast-food — are filled by promoting experienced food and beverage preparation and service workers. Waiters, waitresses, chefs, and fast-food workers demonstrating potential for handling increased responsibility sometimes advance to assistant manager or management trainee jobs. Executive chefs need extensive experience working as chefs, and general managers need prior restaurant experience, usually as assistant managers.

A bachelor's degree in restaurant and food service management provides particularly strong preparation for a career in this occupation. Almost 1,000 colleges and universities offer 4-year programs in restaurant and hospitality management or institutional food service management; a growing number of university programs offer graduate degrees in hospitality management or similar fields. For those not interested in pursuing a 4-year degree, community and junior colleges, technical institutes, and other institutions offer programs in the field leading to an associate degree or other formal certification. Both 2- and 4-year programs provide instruction in subjects such as nutrition, sanitation, and food planning and preparation, as well as accounting,

NATURE OF WORK

business law and management, and computer science. Some programs combine classroom and laboratory study with internships providing on-the-job experience. In addition, many educational institutions offer culinary programs in food preparation. Such training can lead to a career as a cook or chef and provide a foundation for advancement to an executive chef position. Many larger food service operations will provide, or offer to pay for, technical training, such as computer or business courses, so that employees can acquire the business skills necessary to read a spreadsheet or understand the concepts and practices of running a business. Generally, this requires a long-term commitment on the employee's part to both the employer and to the profession.

Most restaurant chains and food service management companies have rigorous training programs for management positions. Through a combination of classroom and on-the-job training, trainees receive instruction and gain work experience in all aspects of the operation of a restaurant or institutional food service facility. Areas include food preparation, nutrition, sanitation, security, company policies and procedures, personnel management, recordkeeping, and preparation of reports. Training on use of the restaurant's computer system is increasingly important as well. Usually, after 6 months or a year, trainees receive their first permanent assignment as an assistant manager.

Most employers emphasize personal qualities when hiring managers. For example, self-discipline, initiative, and leadership ability are essential. Managers must be able to solve problems and concentrate on details. They need good communication skills to deal with customers and suppliers, as well as to motivate and direct their staff. A neat and clean appearance is important, because managers must convey self-confidence and show respect in dealing with the public. Because

NATURE OF WORK

food service management can be physically demanding, good health and stamina are important.

The certified Foodservice Management Professional (FMP) designation is a measure of professional achievement for food service managers. Although not a requirement for employment or advancement in the occupation, voluntary certification provides recognition of professional competence, particularly for managers who acquired their skills largely on the job. The National Restaurant Association Educational Foundation awards the FMP designation to managers who achieve a qualifying score on a written examination, complete a series of courses that cover a range of food service management topics, and meet standards of work experience in the field.

Willingness to relocate often is essential for advancement to positions with greater responsibility. Managers typically advance to larger establishments or regional management positions within restaurant chains. Some eventually open their own food service establishments.

Becoming a Better Manager

Would you like to become a better manager? What can you do to make that happen? Here are some ideas on how to become a better manager.

Training. Get more training. Learn how to use new machines you have in your restaurant or try learning new methods on things you already do. Go to seminars and workshops to learn more about managing your employees. Learn as much as you can about sales, marketing, and advertising.

Get to know your employees better. Sometimes becoming better at what you do requires taking a step back and making sure you know your team.

Find out what they like and do not like about the way the restaurant is being run. Find out if they have any suggestions or things they would like to see changed. You may not know what to change until you ask. Make sure your employees know they will not be in trouble for bringing anything they feel needs evaluation to you so they are more apt to talk openly to you.

Education. You may decide to go to (or back to) school for some additional education. Maybe there are new procedures or techniques you need to learn or you just want to learn something new. Find a class and sign up.

Be a guest. Visit your restaurant as a customer and see how it turns out. You may learn that some things just are not working or maybe you will see some problem area that you would not have spotted before.

Ask for feedback. Ask the other managers or the owner of the business what they think about your management. They may see something they feel you could work on. It never hurts to ask and you may learn something important.

Join an association. Join your state restaurant association. You can always learn from the other managers who are also members. Associations also provide a lot of helpful resources for members. For a list of state restaurant associations, along with contact information for each, see the appendix. Here is the contact information for the National Restaurant Association. They have many resources, links, and research available to you.

> National Restaurant Association
> 1200 17th St.
> NW Washington, DC 20036
> Phone: 202-331-5900
> Web site: **www.restaurant.org**

There are also many resources you can read and review which I have provided in the appendix. I highly recommend that you always strive to be a better manager. There are always things you can learn and ways to make things better.

Conclusion

What an amazing experience writing this book has been. I am so very thankful to all the managers who participated. They took time to answer a very long questionnaire, which covered as many areas as possible that you would want to know about, and provided photos and contact information on each of their restaurants. I hope you have learned much from these wonderful people. I know I did. As I sat writing this and reading their stories and looking at the photos of their restaurants (and food in some cases), I found myself ready to plan a trip to each of the places where they are located. They all sound so wonderful to be at and the best thing is that they all are so different.

No matter what type of restaurant you manage or own, the basics of being a successful manager are the same. Hopefully you have gained much knowledge from the pages of this book and are now ready to go and put some of these ideas and techniques into practice. Good luck and happy managing!

Appendix A

Alphabetical Listing of Featured Restaurants

94th Squadron Restaurant

Mansoor Zia
5240 Paint Branch Parkway
College Park, MD 20740
gmunit44@srcmail.com
www.src.com
T: 301-699-9400
F: 301-779-2305

Altitudes Bar & Grill

Paul Joerger and Lynda Fleischer-Joerger
Two S. Beaver, Suite 2
Flagstaff, AZ 86001
paulyndaj@infomagic.com
T: 928-214-8218
F: 928-773-0414

Avenue Diner

Heather Chell
105 8th Avenue SW Calgary, AB T2P 1B4
Canada
info@avenuediner.com
www.avenuediner.com
T: 403-263-2673
F: 403-266-2674

Bali Wine Bar & Grill

Putu Knutte
2416 18th Street
Sacramento, CA 95818
Baligrill@Sbcglobal.net
www.baligrill.net
T: 916-444-1247

BIN 239

Kelly Keller
239 N. Marina St.
Prescott, AZ 86301
winegeeks@bin239.com
www.bin239.com
T: 928-445-3855
F: 928-445-9264

Bon Appetit at the Art Institute of Chicago
Kristopher Kotte
111 South Michigan Avenue
Chicago, IL 60603
Kris.Kotte@cafebonappetit.com
www.artic.edu / bamco.com
T: 312-443-7274
F: 312-263-0697

Bubba's Roadhouse & Saloon
Jay Johnson
2121 SW Pine Island Road
Cape Coral, FL 33991
bubbasroadhouse@excite.com
www.bubbasroadhouse.net
T: 239-282-5520
F: 239-282-5523

Celebration Banquets and Catering & Chicago's Deep Dish 'N Dogs (Restaurant)
Joseff A. VanHorn
2121 Celebration Dr.
Grand Rapids, MI 49519
jvanhorn@celebrationcinema.com
www.celebrationbanquets.com
T: 616-447-4200 ext. 1355
F: 616-447-4201

Gastone A. Zampieri

P.O. Box 1853
Belize City, Belize, Central America
giotto1@msn.com

Haro Tapas & Pintxos

Chef Gina Marie Onorato
2436 S. Oakley
Chicago, IL. 60608
chefginamarie@aol.com
www.harotapas.com
T: 773-329-5515

Kalenuik Food Services, Inc.

Ron Kalenuik
240 Wade Ave. W.
Penticton, BC, Canada,
V2A-1T8
chefk@chefk.com
www.chefk.com
T: 250-492-7383
F: 250-493-4815

Lagniappe (A Creole Cajun Joynt)

Mary Madison
1525 West 79th Street
Chicago, IL 60620
Lagniappe26@aol.com
www.cajunjoynt.com
T: 773-994-6375
F: 773-285-9001

Le Bistro

Elin Trousdale
4626 North Federal Highway
Lighthouse Point, Florida 33064
andyelin@bellsouth.net
www.lebistrorestaurant.com
T: 954-946-9240

Leila Restaurant

Roy B. Assad
120 S. Dixie Highway
West Palm Beach, FL 33401
roy@leilawpb.com
www.leilawpb.com
T: 561-659-7373
F: 561-833-9417

MCBP Enterprises, Inc / My Turn Pub
Sue Paulson
www.myturnpub.com

Ninety-Nine Restaurant
Stephanie Morley
20 MacArthur Blvd.
Coventry, RI 02816
Smorin11@cox.net
T: 401-615-1673

One-Eyed Jack's Restaurant & Saloon
Michael Larey
1201 Dixie Overland Rd.
Bossier City, LA 71111
michaellarey@one-eyedjacks.net
www.one-eyedjacks.net
T: 318-549-4990
F: 318-549-4992

Peppercorns Restaurant
Paul Barthel
877 Geneva Road
Carol Streem, IL 60188
paulbarthel@comcast.net
peppercornsrestaurant.org
T: 630-871-7636
C: 708-715-3927
F: 630-690-2969

Remember That Chef, In Home Dining & Personal Chef Services
Jaime Miller
40 Grandville Ave. Suite, 1510 Hamilton, Ontario L8E 1J7
Jaime@rememberthatchef.ca
www.rememberthatchef.ca
T: 905-560-6924
F: 905-560-9795

San Delico, Inc.
Nazir N. Khamisa
P.O. Box 477
Kirkland, WA 98083
nazirk@comcast.net
T: 206-227-7750
F: 206-770-8925

St. Bernard's School

Carolyn Wells

4 East 98th St.

NYC, NY 10129

wellsc690@aol.com

www.saintbernards.org

T: 212-289-7879

F: 212-010-6628

The Union League Club of Chicago

Paul Petrulis

65 West Jackson Blvd, Suite 911

Chicago, IL 60604

petrulis@ulcc.org

www.ulcc.org

T: 312-427-7800 ext. 430

Timothy O'Toole's Pub

Humberto Martinez Jr.

622 N. Fairbanks Ct.

Chicago, IL 60611

Pub622@sbcglobal.net

www.timothyotooles.com

T: 312-642-0700

F: 312-642-6848

Trattoria Bella

Daniel Pace
6 Radcliffe Drive
Moosic, PA 18507
tbella@trattoriabella.com
www.trattoriabella.com
T: 570-961-2250
F: 570-341-5241

Uncorked ~ The Unpretentious Wine Bar

Ali Amundson
16427 N. Scottsdale Rd. Ste.130
Scottsdale, AZ 85254
www.uncorkedwinebar.com
T: 480-699-9230
F: 480-699-9239

Appendix B

Restaurant Industry Facts

2007 RESTAURANT INDUSTRY OVERVIEW	
Sales	$537 billion
Locations	935,000 — serving more than 70 billion meal and snack occasions
Employees	12.8 million — the industry is the largest employer besides the government

SALES PROJECTIONS		
Restaurant Industry Sales	Type of Establishment	2007 Estimated Sales in billions
$536.9 / $322.5 / $199.7 / $42.8 — 1970 1987 1997 2007* *projected	Commercial Eating Places	$491
	Drinking Places	$363
	Managed	$16
	Services	$36
	Lodging-place Restaurants	$27
	Rental, Vending, Recreation, Mobile	$49
	Other	$46

2007 RESTAURANT INDUSTRY OVERVIEW
CORNERSTONE OF OUR NATION'S ECONOMY

Restaurant-industry sales are forecast to advance 5% in 2007 and equal 4% of the U.S. gross domestic product.

The overall economic impact of the restaurant industry is expected to exceed $1.3 trillion in 2007, including sales in related industries, such as agriculture, transportation, and manufacturing.

Every dollar spent by consumers in restaurants generates an additional $2.34 spent in other industries allied with the restaurant industry.

Every additional $1 million in restaurant sales generates an additional 37 jobs for the nation's economy.

Average unit sales in 2004 were $795,000 at full service restaurants and $671,000 at limited-service restaurants.

The average household expenditure for food away from home in 2005 was $2,634, or $1,054 per person.

More than seven out of 10 eating-and-drinking places are single-unit (independent) operations.

NUMBER ONE EMPLOYER

The restaurant industry employs an estimated 12.8 million people, making it the nation's largest employer outside of the government.

Eating-and-drinking places are extremely labor-intensive. Sales per full-time-equivalent employee were $57,032 in 2005 and notably lower than other industries.

The restaurant industry provides work for more than 9 percent of those employed in the United States.

The restaurant industry provides work for more than 9 percent of those employed in the United States.

The restaurant industry is expected to add 2 million jobs over the next decade, for total employment of 14.8 million in 2017.

2007 RESTAURANT INDUSTRY OVERVIEW

Nearly half of all adults have worked in the restaurant industry at some time during their lives and 32 percent of adults got their first job experience in a restaurant.

THE TYPICAL EMPLOYEE IN A FOOD SERVICE OCCUPATION IS:

Female (55 percent)

Under 30 years of age (53 percent)

Working part-time and averaging 25 hours a week

Living in a household with two or more wage earners (79 percent)

Ladder to Management Opportunity

Women and minorities represent three of five owners of eating and drinking place firms, compared to less than half of all U.S. firms.

One-quarter of eating and drinking place firms are owned by women, 15% by Asians, 8% by Hispanics, and 4% by African-Americans.

The number of food service managers is projected to increase 11 percent form 2007 to 2017.

Roughly three out of five food service managers have annual household incomes of $50,000 or more.

Three out of five first-line supervisors of food preparation and service workers in 2005 were women, 16 percent were of Hispanic origin, and 14 percent were African-American.

Two out of five quick service operators will increase the proportion of their budget allocated to training in 2007.

Nearly half of all adults have worked in the restaurant industry at some point during their lives, and 32 percent of adults got their first job experience in a restaurant.

RESTAURANTS BY THE NUMBERS

$1.5 billion	Restaurant-industry sales on a typical day in 2007

2007 RESTAURANT INDUSTRY OVERVIEW

57 percent	Percent of customers who would use delivery to their home or office if offered by table service restaurants.
4 out of 5	Consumers agree that going out to a restaurant is a better way to use their leisure time than cooking and cleaning up.
38 percent	Percentage of table service-restaurant operators who anticipate that takeout will represent a larger proportion of their total sales in 2007.
43 percent	Percent of table service restaurant operators offering organic menu items who anticipate that they will represent a larger proportion of their total sales in 2007.
37 percent	Percent of consumers who have used curbside takeout at a table service restaurant.
59 percent	Percent of table service restaurant operators that offer televisions for customer entertainment.

*Chart information courtesy of the National Restaurant Association, **http:// www.restaurant.org/research/ind_glance.cfm**. Printed with permission.*

Appendix C

Charts and Graphs

Length of Time in Management

1-5 years ▓6-10 years ☐11-15 years ☐16-20 years ▨21 + years

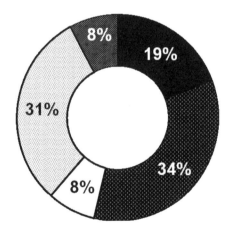

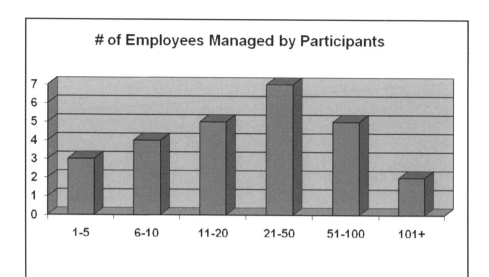

# of Employees Managed by Participants

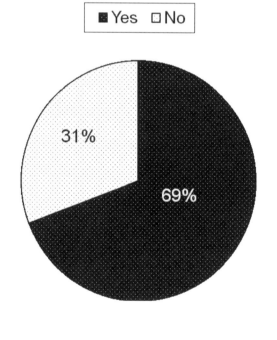

Do the Participants Own their Own Restaurant?

■ Yes □ No

31%

69%

Do the Participants Serve Alcohol?

■ Yes ▣ No ▢ Not Yet

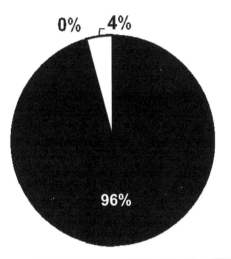

0%   4%

96%

Do the Participants Use Fresh or Frozen Foods?

▢ Fresh ▣ Frozen ■ Both

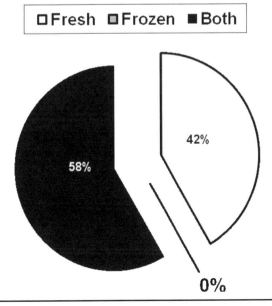

42%

58%

0%

Do the Participants Offer Catering Services?

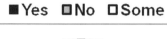

■ Yes ☐ No ☐ Some

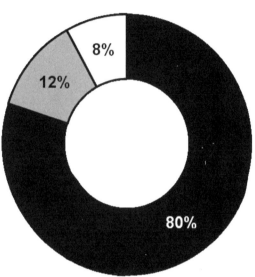

8%

12%

80%

Do the Participants Accept Reservations?

■ Yes ☐ No ■ Some ☐ Call Ahead

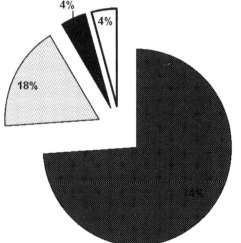

4%

4%

18%

Do the Managers Use Flex Scheduling?

■Yes ▣No ▢Some

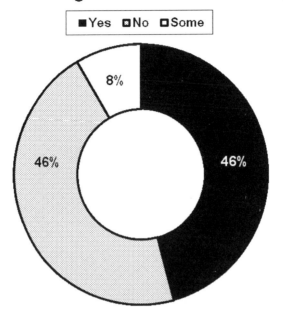

Do the Managers Offer Coupons in Advertising?

▢Yes ■No ▣Some

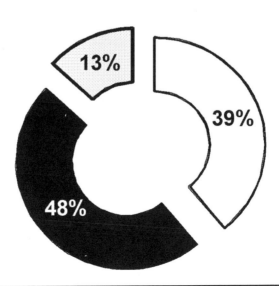

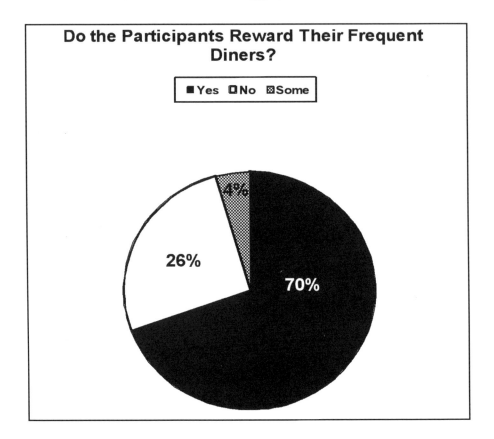

Appendix D

State Restaurant Association Listing

Alabama Restaurant Association
PO Box 241413
Montgomery, AL 36124-1413
Phone: (334) 244-1320
Web site: **www.stayandplayalabama.com**

Alaska Cabaret, Hotel, Restaurant & Retailers Association (CHARR)
1111 E 80th Ave
Ste 3
Anchorage, AK 99518-3312
Phone: (907) 274-8133
Web site: **www.alaskacharr.com**

Arizona Restaurant & Hospitality Association
2400 N Central Ave
Ste 109
Phoenix, AZ 85004-1300
Phone: (602) 307-9134
Web site: **www.azrestaurant.org**

Arkansas Hospitality Association
PO Box 3866
Little Rock, AR 72203-3866
Phone: (501) 376-2323
Web site: **www.arhospitality.org**

California Restaurant Association
1011 10th St
Sacramento, CA 95814-3501
Phone: (916) 447-5793
Web site: **www.calrest.org**

Colorado Restaurant Association
430 E 7th Ave
Denver, CO 80203-3605
Phone: (303) 830-2972
Web site: **www.coloradorestaurant.com**

Connecticut Restaurant Association
100 Roscommon Dr
Suite 320
Middletown, CT 06457-7559
Phone: (860) 635-3334
Web site: **www.ctrestaurant.org**

Delaware Restaurant Association
PO Box 8004
Newark, DE 19714-8004
Phone: (302) 738-2545
Web site: **www.dineoutdelaware.com**

Florida Restaurant & Lodging Association
PO Box 1779
Tallahassee, FL 32302-1779
Phone: (850) 224-2250
Web site: **www.frla.org**

Georgia Restaurant Association
480 E Paces Ferry Rd NE
Suite 7
Atlanta, GA 30305-3324
Phone: (404) 467-9000
Web site: **www.garestaurants.org**

Hawaii Restaurant Association

1451 S King St
Suite 503
Honolulu, HI 96814-2509
Phone: (808) 944-9105
Web site: **www.hawaiirestaurants.org**

Idaho Lodging & Restaurant Association

PO Box 1822
Boise, ID 83701-1822
Phone: (208) 342-0010

Illinois Restaurant Association

33 W Monroe St Ste 250
Chicago, IL 60603-5300
Phone: (312) 787-4000
Web site: **www.illinoisrestaurants.org**

Restaurant & Hospitality Association of Indiana

200 S Meridian St
Ste 350
Indianapolis, IN 46225-1076
Phone: (317) 673 4211
Web site: **www.indianarestaurants.org**

Iowa Restaurant Association

8525 Douglas Ave
Ste 47
Des Moines, IA 50322-2929
Phone: (515) 276-1454
Web site: **www.iowahospitality.com**

Kansas Restaurant & Hospitality Association

3500 N Rock Rd Bldg 1300
Wichita, KS 67226-1335
Phone: (316) 267-8383
Web site: **www.krha.org**

Kentucky Restaurant Association

133 N Evergreen Rd
Suite 201
Louisville, KY 40243-1484
Phone: (502) 896-0464
Web site: **www.kyra.org**

Louisiana Restaurant Association

2700 N Arnoult Rd
Metairie, LA 70002-5916
Phone: (504) 454-2277
Web site: **www.lra.org**

Maine Restaurant Association

PO Box 5060

Augusta, ME 04332-5060

Phone: (207) 623-2178

Web site: **www.mainerestaurant.com**

Restaurant Association of Maryland

6301 Hillside Ct

Columbia, MD 21046-1048

Phone: (410) 290-6800

Web site: **www.marylandrestaurants.com**

Massachusetts Restaurant Association

333 Turnpike Rd

Ste 102

Southborough Technology Park

Southborough, MA 01772-1755

Phone: (508) 303-9905

Web site: **www.marestaurantassoc.org**

Michigan Restaurant Association

225 W Washtenaw St

Lansing, MI 48933-1533

Phone: (517) 482-5244

Web site: **www.michiganrestaurant.org**

Minnesota Restaurant Association

305 Roselawn Ave E

Saint Paul, MN 55117-2031

Phone: (651) 778-2400

Web site: **www.hospitalitymn.com**

Mississippi Hospitality & Restaurant Association

130 Riverview Dr

Suite A

Flowood, MS 39232-8921

Phone: (601) 420-4210

Web site: **www.msra.org**

Missouri Restaurant Association

1810 Craig Rd

Ste 225

Saint Louis, MO 63146-4761

Phone: (314) 576-2777

Web site: **www.morestaurants.org**

Montana Restaurant Association

1645 Parkhill Dr Ste 6

Billings, MT 59102-3067

Phone: (406) 256-1005

Web site: **www.mtretail.com**

Nebraska Restaurant Association & Hospitality Education Foundation

1610 S 70th St
Suite 101
Lincoln, NE 68506-1565
Phone: (402) 488-3999
Web site: **www.nebraska-dining.org**

Nevada Restaurant Association

1500 E Tropicana Ave
Suite 114-A
Las Vegas, NV 89119-6514
Phone: (702) 878-2313
Web site: **www.nvrestaurants.com**

New Hampshire Lodging & Restaurant Association

PO Box 1175
Concord, NH 03302-1175
Phone: (603) 228-9585
Web site: **www.nhlra.com**

New Jersey Restaurant Association

126 W State St
Trenton, NJ 08608-1102
Phone: (609) 599-3316
Web site: **www.njra.org**

New Mexico Restaurant Association
9201 Montgomery Blvd NE
Suite 602
Albuquerque, NM 87111-2470
Phone: (505) 343-9848
Web site: **www.nmrestaurants.org**

New York State Restaurant Association
409 New Karner Rd
Albany, NY 12205-3883
Phone: (518) 452-4222
Web site: **www.nysra.org**

North Carolina Restaurant and Lodging Association
6036 Six Forks Rd
Raleigh, NC 27609-3899
Phone: (919) 844-0098
Web site: **www.ncra.org**

North Dakota State Hospitality Association
804 E Main Ave
Bismarck, ND 58501-4526
Phone: (701) 223-3313
Web site: **www.ndhospitality.com**

Ohio Restaurant Association
1525 Bethel Rd
Ste 301
Columbus, OH 43220-2054
Phone: (614) 442-3535
Web site: **www.ohiorestaurant.org**

Oklahoma Restaurant Association
3800 N Portland Ave
Oklahoma City, OK 73112-2994
Phone: (405) 942-8181
Web site: **www.okrestaurants.com**

Oregon Restaurant Association
8565 SW Salish Lane
Ste 120
Wilsonville, OR 97070-9633
Phone: (503) 682-4422
Web site: **www.ora.org**

Pennsylvania Restaurant Association
100 State St
Harrisburg, PA 17101-1034
Phone: (717) 232-4433
Web site: **www.parestaurant.org**

Rhode Island Hospitality & Tourism Association
94 Sabra St
Cranston, RI 02910-1031
Phone: (401) 223-1120
Web site: **www.rihospitality.org**

Hospitality Association of South Carolina
PO Box 7577
1005 Gervais St
Columbia, SC 29202-7577
Phone: (803) 765-9000
Web site: **www.schospitality.org**

South Dakota Retailers Association Restaurant Division
PO Box 638
320 E Capitol
Pierre, SD 57501-0638
Phone: (605) 224-5050
Web site: **www.sdra.org**

Tennessee Restaurant Association
PO Box 681207
Franklin, TN 37068-1207
Phone: (615) 771-7056
Web site: **www.thetra.com**

Texas Restaurant Association

PO Box 1429
Austin, TX 78767-1429
Phone: (512) 457-4100
Web site: **www.restaurantville.com**

Utah Restaurant Association

515 S 700 E Street
Ste 3D
Salt Lake City, UT 84102
Phone: (801) 322-0123
Web site: **www.utahdineout.com**

Vermont Hospitality Council

PO Box 37
Montpelier, VT 05601-0037
Phone: (802) 223-2636
Web site: **www.vtchamber.com**

Virginia Hospitality & Travel Association

2101 Libbie Ave
Richmond, VA 23230-2621
Phone: (804) 288-3065
Web site: **www.vhta.org**

Washington Restaurant Association
510 Plum St SE
Ste 200
Olympia, WA 98501-1587
Phone: (360) 956-7279
Web site: **www.wrahome.com**

Restaurant Association Metropolitan Washington
1200 17th St NW
Suite 100
Washington, DC 20036-3010
Phone: (202) 331-5990
Web site: **www.ramw.org**

West Virginia Hospitality and Travel Association
PO Box 2391
Charleston, WV 25328-2391
Phone: (304) 342-6511
Web site: **www.wvhta.com**

Wisconsin Restaurant Association
2801 Fish Hatchery Rd
Madison, WI 53713-3197
Phone: (608) 270-9950
Web site: **www.wirestaurant.org**

Wyoming Lodging & Restaurant Association

PO Box 1003

Cheyenne, WY 82003-1003

Phone: (307) 634-8816

Web site: **www.wlra.org**

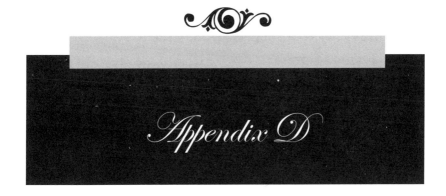

Appendix D

Restaurant Web Sites:

Eldred Training and Development: **www.eldtrain.com.au**

Foodservice.com: **www.foodservice.com**

FoodserviceCentral: **www.foodservicecentral.com**

National Restaurant Association: **www.restaurant.org**

Profitable Hospitality: **www.profitablehospitality.com**

RestaurantOwner.com: **www.restaurantowner.com**

Restaurant Marketing Group: **www.restaurantmarketinggroup.org**

RestaurantReport: **www.restaurantreport.com**

The Restaurant Doctor: **www.restaurantdoctor.com**

Web Articles:

http://ezinearticles.com/?Six-Ways-To-Attract-New-Customers-To-Your-Restaurant&id=3669

http://www.articlealley.com/article_43416_64.html

http://www.restaurantreport.com/departments/biz_greater_expectations.html

http://www.articlealley.com/article_101954_36.html

Books:

These books come from Atlantic Publishing Company, **www.atlantic-pub.com**. Atlantic is the leading resource for food service books and resources. These are also all available in eBook format on their Web site.

The Restaurant Manager's Handbook: How to Set Up, Operate, and Manage a Financially Successful Food Service Operation — With Companion CD-ROM (Completely Revised 4th Edition, Item # RMH-04)

The Encyclopedia of Restaurant Forms: A Complete Kit of Ready-to-Use Checklists, Worksheets, and Training Aids for a Successful Food Service Operation — With Companion CD-ROM (Item # ERF-02)

The Encyclopedia of Restaurant Training: A Complete Ready-to-Use Training Program for All Positions in the Food Service Industry — With Companion CD-ROM (Item # ERT-02)

The Responsible Serving of Alcoholic Beverages: A Complete Staff Training Course for Bars, Restaurants, and Caterers — With Companion CD-ROM (Item # RSA-01)

The Waiter & Waitress and Wait Staff Training Handbook: A Complete Guide to the Proper Steps in Service for Food & Beverage Employees (Item #WWT-TH or Spanish Item #WWT-SP)

The Food Service Manager's Guide to Creative Cost-Cutting and Cost Control: Over 2,001 Innovative and Simple Ways to Save Your Food Service Operation Thousands By Reducing Expenses — With Companion CD-ROM (Item # CCC-01)

The Professional Bar & Beverage Manager's Handbook: How to Open and Operate a Financially Successful Bar, Tavern, and Night Club — With Companion CD-ROM (Item # PBB-01)

The Professional Caterer's Handbook: How to Open and Operate a Financially Successful Catering Business — With Companion CD-ROM (Item # PCH-01)

The Non-Commercial Food Service Manager's Handbook: A Complete Guide for Hospitals, Nursing Homes, Military, Prisons, Schools, and Churches: With Companion CD-ROM (Item # NCF-02)

The Restaurant Dream? (Item # TRD-01)

HACCP & Sanitation in Restaurants and Food Service Operations: A Practical Guide Based on the USDA Food Code — With Companion CD-ROM (Item #HSR-02)

365 Ways to Motivate and Reward Your Employees Every Day — With Little or No Money (Item # 365-01)

Superior Customer Service: How to Keep Customers Racing Back to Your Business — Time-Tested Examples from Leading Companies (Item # SCS-01)

How To Hire, Train, and KEEP The Best Employees For your Small Business — With Companion CD-ROM (Item #HTK-02)

365 Low Or No Cost Workplace Teambuilding Activities: Games and Exercises Designed to Build Trust and Encourage Teamwork Among Employees (Item #LCW-01)

365 Foolish Mistakes Smart Managers Make Every Day: How and Why to Avoid Them (Item # FMS-02)

199 Pre-Written Employee Performance Appraisals: The Complete Guide to Successful Employee Evaluations and Documentation — With Companion CD-ROM (Item # EPP-02)

The Food Service Professional Guide to Restaurant Marketing & Advertising: For Just A Few Dollars A Day (Item # FS3-01)

The Food Service Professional Guide to Restaurant Promotion & Publicity: For Just A Few Dollars A Day (Item # FS4-01)

The Food Service Professional Guide to Controlling Restaurant & Food Service Operating Costs (Item # FS5-01)

The Food Service Professional Guide to Controlling Restaurant & Food Service Food Costs (Item # FS6-01)

The Food Service Professional Guide to Controlling Restaurant & Food Service Labor Costs (Item # FS7-01)

The Food Service Professional Guide to Controlling Liquor Wine & Beverage Costs (Item # FS8-01)

The Food Service Professional Guide to Building Restaurant Profits: How to Ensure Maximum Results (Item # FS9-01)

The Food Service Professional Guide to Waiter and Waitress Training How to Develop Your Staff For Maximum Service and Profit (Item # FS10-01 or Spanish Version Item # FS10-SP)

The Food Service Professional Guide to Bar and Beverage Operation Ensuring Success and Maximum Profit (Item # FS11-01)

*The Food Service Professional Guide to Increasing Restaurant Sales: Boost Your Sales & Profits By Selling More Appetizers, Desserts, & Side Item*s (Item # FS15-01)

Other Resources

Food Safety Poster Series (Set of 16) (Item #FSP-PS) — **www.atlantic-pub.com**

Author Biography

Angela C. Adams is the award-winning author of *The eBay Success Chronicles*, her first book. Now, putting her B.A. degree in Communications to use, she has written another book on successful people — this time in the area of restaurant management.

Angela freelances in writing and design services, as well as working her full-time job as the Managing Editor of Atlantic Publishing Company in Ocala, Florida.

Angela resides in Ocala with her boyfriend, Dennis, and her kitten, Panda. Besides her work, she also enjoys reading, writing, and spending time with her friends.

You can find out more about Angela on her Web site: **www.ACAFreelance. com**. You can contact her at **angela.c.adams@hotmail.com**.

Index

FOOD SERVICE MANAGEMENT:
HOW TO SUCCEED IN THE HIGH-RISK RESTAURANT BUSINESS — BY SOMEONE WHO DID

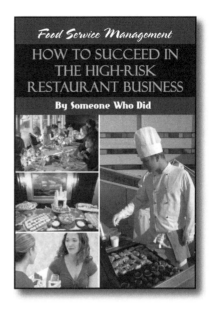

Bill Wentz, speaks from experience, making his advice that much more valuable. Wentz truly understands the industry and shares the priceless experiences he had and lessons he learned throughout his career. In this book, you will learn if a food service career is right for you, the many opportunities available in the industry, and where to go for the best training. Food service managers will learn how to predict food costs, how to achieve profit goals, how to conduct recipe cost analysis, and how to realistically price a menu. In addition, this book discusses labor costs and controls, profit and loss statements, accounting systems, inventory, sanitation, and effective communication.

Whether you are considering a career in food services or you are already the manager of an establishment, you will certainly find some wisdom in Wentz's words. Wentz passes on his knowledge in this easy-to-read and entertaining book that not only tells you how to survive in the food service business but also tells you how to be successful.

ISBN-13: 978-1-60138-024-1
288 Pages • $24.95

HOW TO OPEN & OPERATE A FINANCIALLY SUCCESSFUL PERSONAL CHEF BUSINESS: WITH COMPANION CD-ROM

A personal chef offers a professional service of meal preparation. A client's individual tastes drive the creation of their customized menu. These personalized meals are prepared either in the client's home or your catering kitchen and then packaged, labeled, possibly delivered, and stored in the refrigerator or freezer. Most services include complete grocery shopping, customized menu planning, and storage in oven/microwavable containers. Families in which both spouses work, singles and couples who work long, hard hours, seniors who would rather not or cannot cook anymore, gourmets who love to cook but who do not always have the time, and individuals that have medical conditions, such as wheat/gluten intolerance, milk or other sensitivities, diabetes, or high blood pressure, who require specialized meals will seek your services.

The book covers the entire process of a personal chef business from startup to ongoing management in an easy to understand way, pointing out methods to increase your chances of success and showing you how to avoid the common mistakes that can doom a startup.

ISBN-13: 978-1-60138-141-5
288 Pages • $39.95

To order call 1-800-814-1132 or visit www.atlantic-pub.com

THE RESTAURANT MANAGER'S HANDBOOK: HOW TO SET UP, OPERATE AND MANAGE A FINANCIALLY SUCCESSFUL FOOD SERVICE OPERATION — WITH COMPANION CD-ROM

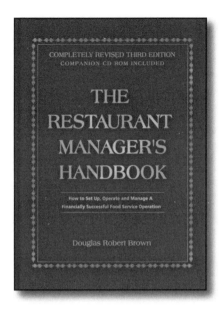

According to the Occupational This comprehensive 1,000-page book will show you step by step how to set up, operate, and manage a financially successful food service operation. The book covers the entire process of a restaurant startup and ongoing management in an easy-to-understand way, pointing out methods to increase your chances of success and showing how to avoid common mistakes. The CD-ROM contains all the forms in the book. The extensive resource guide details over 7,000 suppliers to the industry.

"The essence of a successful handbook — no jokes and preachy lectures; just the facts. If you're currently running a restaurant and afraid to appear inadequate, load the CD-ROM and pretend you're checking your e-mail while figuring out the monthly audit procedures. The next time your favorite kitchen runs short of the special or closes for a lack of permit, serve them this great reference book."

— *Writers Notes Magazine*

ISBN-10: 0-910627-97-5 • ISBN-13: 978-0-910627-97-9
1,000 Pages • $79.95

DID YOU BORROW THIS COPY?

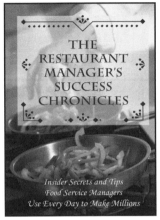

THE RESTAURANT MANAGER'S SUCCESS CHRONICLES

Insider Secrets and Tips
Food Service Managers
Use Every Day to Make Millions

Have you been borrowing a copy of *How to The Restaurant Manager's Success Chronicles: Insider Secrets and Techniques Food Service Managers Use Every Day to Make Millions* from a friend, colleague, or library? Wouldn't you like your own copy for quick and easy reference? To order, photocopy the form below and send to:

Atlantic Publishing Company
1405 SW 6th Ave • Ocala, FL 34471-0640